"IT" IS God

NOT WHO IS GOD,
BUT WHAT IS GOD

Lois B. Mayette

Author's Tranquility Press
ATLANTA, GEORGIA

Copyright © 2024 by Lois B. Mayette

All rights reserved. No part of this publication may be reproduced, distributed or transmitted in any form or by any means, including photocopying, recording, or other electronic or mechanical methods, without the prior written permission of the publisher, except in the case of brief quotations embodied in critical reviews and certain other noncommercial uses permitted by copyright law. For permission requests, write to the publisher, addressed "Attention: Permissions Coordinator," at the address below.

Lois B. Mayette/Author's Tranquility Press
3900 N Commerce Dr. Suite 300 #1255
Atlanta, GA 30344, USA
www.authorstranquilitypress.com

Ordering Information:
Quantity sales. Special discounts are available on quantity purchases by corporations, associations, and others. For details, contact the "Special Sales Department" at the address above.

It Is God: Not Who Is God, But What Is God / Lois B. Mayette
Paperback: 978-1-965075-41-8
eBook: 978-1-965075-42-5

Contents

Preface vii

"It" 1

Culturally 7

Authorities 9

So what is God rather than who is God? 18

Family Structure 24

Emotions 27

Buddhism/Christianity 31

Marriage of Science and Religion 37

Albert Einstein 39

Spirituality 42

Death/Dying 59

God is Unconditional Love 67

My Daughter 109

Preface

There are many reasons for compiling these writings. First and foremost is to formulate my own beliefs.

Secondly, to share them with you. Thirdly to perhaps help you see how growth and development happens for the individual as well as a culture.

Many religions have been controlling the masses by using fear of God rather than the unconditional love of God. God is unconditional love.

Religion and Spirituality are not the same. Religion has kept us apart from God and Spirituality will give you a personal relationship with God. We are one and made in God's image.

I want to introduce you to a new mindset by using "It" as God and removing the emotional human traits for God.

Some may see this as a disrespect for God but it is not. It is just an example of how our old beliefs of God were not sound. Unconditional love takes away all rules of good/bad, right/wrong, and erases all high achy in heaven or earth. Think of parenting, if any member dominates than there is going to be an imbalance and unconditional love would not be there.

"It" in the dictionary is defined as an impersonal force, taking no sides or meaning for me having no emotional human traits. Emotions are learned but feeling are innate but can be squashed or fostered in our early experiences. That is why parenting is one of the most important jobs in the world. We chose to see the Father in God for that reason. Now it is time to move God into neither male or female but God is omni present, potent and omniscient. Mankind is not. So what is God? What do we have that is God like?

Jesus taught by examples and lessons. I hope to help us understand the omni of God and how to tap into being more God like. Unconditional Love.

Einstein said," everything is energy or it is nothing."

So what is soul, spirit, essence, aura, and God but energy, as it is in everything, is everywhere, and eternal.

What of you is eternal? The body dies.

Thoughts, words, and deeds are all energy.

This is the emphases in these writings. Change our thinking therefore our feelings and then our behavior.

Behavior can change before feelings as feelings can lag but thinking is the powerhouse.

Let's explore!

"It" is God
Not who is God, what is God

Culturally we want to make God, human and it is not difficult to see how that has created some basic problems for many. He/she is not human for several reasons. "It"/God is not human and is everywhere, in everything, and constant Never ending.

It, in the dictionary is defined as impersonal force. Impersonal is defined as not existing as a person.

So if it is in everything what can it be?

"It" used here is meant to help us step out of our old thinking and mindsets and into an exploring mode rather than settling for outdated teachings which made God human. Bringing God to our level has come with many problems and we are bored with old concepts that do not ring true nor do they advance our beliefs. Look around and see that religion has not advanced our everyday problems and have kept us stuck from advancing from adolescence to community. Actually most wars are about religion. Let's stop this.

If this makes you upset as you liked the father image, I understand but try to follow along as this concept does not change God from being the higher power and can help bring God even closer to you, especially you who did not have a good relationship with your father.

Greater is "It" that is in you than is in the world. This is meant to help you take God to a more realistic idea.

So if God is in everything, what can that be?

Humans cannot be in everything but most of the substances we are made of are in everything. Most humans cannot be everywhere at once. Well most humans cannot without changing their vibrations, which only a few have accomplished. However our spirits/souls does all the time. First clue!

God/ "It" is constant and humans are ever changing and have phases that we go through as we are born an infant, than a tattler, then a preschooler, then go to school and etc. God "It" is constant however experiences through us what we experience. How? God is in us.

What is in us that is God? God is eternal. We have eternal life. We know that the flesh dies as we have witnessed that in our life so what is left? What is common in all of us and God? The spirit, aura, soul, essence and energy.

Take a foreign language and you will call "It" something else. This may help you get out of old mindset and into a new way of thinking. As thinking is the powerhouse. Thoughts are energy. Remember, your prayers are answered before you ask? Well here is why as thoughts are energy before they materialize.

Here is the challenge: Do you want to change your thinking? Do we find all sorts of excuses to stay with the old? Do not have time. How do I know it is the truth anyway?

I can confess that it is a lot of hard work as I have spent all my life in "It". I like that "It" as I now realize that I have always been in God/ "It". My quest for the truth has been long at the task but exciting also.

Remember, the truth shall set you free". Our task for life is to be set free. How? To find the truth. Whose truth? what truth? Let's call it revolving truth because if you don't know this you will not know that. In other words it is a never-ending process of ever-changing truths. Truths for your today.

Discovery has always been a human quest and can be very exciting. You are really not discovering anything new as it was always there from the beginning of time. You might say you are remembering it as you also were there at the beginning of time. This is what makes you and God/ "It" spirit one or God in you. It is also why it is necessary to go within. It is very hard to find time to go within with mass media and busy schedules to direct us in the likely wrong direction I am of the generation that grew up with no phone or TV. I feel very lucky as it left us to use our creativity. It is not out there it is within that we find the truth, our truth as this journey is not about the others it is about you. Setting yourself apart is not easy but necessary.

The answers are within. Even churches did not do a very good job at teaching what is meant by going within. I did not find my spiritual life from churches where I spent 60 plus years. Churches are perhaps a good foundation but living on a foundation can be unfulfilling and did not answer my spiritual questions or help me find a personal relationship with God. If we are to become more Christ like and he had a deep personal relationship with God, it has to be personal. You need to know and hear that still small voice. My sheep will know my voice. I believe I knew it very young It wasn't something you talked about as no one else seemed too.

Like your education in anything it is a foundation and much of it is history of where churches came from and where they might go or need to go. Churches became their own demise as they stayed in old dogma, which becomes very unsettling after awhile. God is now in the 21st century with us. At this time in our history we should have more answers than not. Some have answers but it is not widespread. The phenomenon that happens when you discover a truth is that you can't keep it to yourself. You have this great desire to tell it to someone. Did Christ not know this when he told those he healed not to tell anyone for he knew they would. In my great days of growth I had some people going through it with me and we could share for hours what we were learning. The journey is different for all of us yet the same too. That is because what we need is different. You are a unique, important individual. When you get my age 77 you know more about your purpose for coming to planet earth as you begin to see how it all comes together.

It is impossible to remember everything in one lifetime and that is intended. Intended so we use the experience to understand more fully the thinking, hopefully new thinking about the experience in feelings and behavior.

Everything is about thinking as you change your thinking, you change your feelings and then your behavior.

"It" God experiences everything we experience thru us Everything affects everything else as we are all one so everything is one. Throw a pebble into the water and it affects the whole body of water. You see some of the effects and some you do not. Our oneness is like that. The effect of our behavior may be seen right away some after a while and some not in this life time or at all. When things do not happen right away it is good to see it without time. That is have no need for time in a situation. Know that the process is going on.

I use a puzzle or ladder to see my picture of what is happening in the process. If a piece is missing you will not get the peace that passes all understanding and know that a piece of the puzzle is still missing. That last piece is crucial as it gives the full understanding. We are never ending story, we were there in the creation and we have eternal life which cannot end. You do have new beginnings, however. We call them new souls.

Again it is not the flesh that has eternal life but the spirit, energy, aura, or essence of you. After death you will continue to create and understand more The understanding helps you change the way you see situations and this requires you to put away old thinking and create new concepts. We are made in the likeness of God and none of the likeness is human. That is of the emotions. God does not have needs or emotions but does have feelings. Feelings are different than emotions. Feelings do not need emotional attachments. This is one of the hardest concepts for us, culturally, to understand. People who worry think that they love more than others, that is why they worry but it has nothing to do with love. Love does the opposite, it trusts.

We lump feelings and emotions together as if they are one and the same which they are not. If you are ready do some checking this out.

God/"It" needs nothing from us. How could something that has and created everything need something. Now this is also a big dichotomy, because God does experience life through us, "It" feels our pain without the emotions attached. So God has no needs from us but does experience life through us. He never leaves us or forsake us and is there every step of the way. I experienced anger, sadness, aloneness and etc. without the emotions and no internal change. The gut did not carry the emotions. We were taught in psychology that the lack of emotions was a illness and it is just the opposite, for too much emotions cause illness like panic attacks. At first not having the baggage of emotions is scary as it is like you do not care when you care more but it is your thoughts not gut. Learning to be without emotions helps you make decisions in a situation with clear thinking. Here is an example that stands out for me; a female ran into me totally my car we were both alright and that is what is important not the car. I stood talking to her and her husband as she had to call him as she locked herself out of her SUV and left it running. She was upset about my car and asked, "how I could be so calm and even talk to her?" Even I get amazed when the emotions are put in check. You are not doing the blaming game which is useless at this point as it has happened so deal with it.

Emotions many times cloud the issue and can help make the wrong decisions or jump to the wrong conclusions and that is not what is really happening. We have all been there so work on having feelings without all the emotions. Now one way to get in touch with this concept is to see how our culture told little boys not to have emotions and little girls that it was ok. What happened with our males in our culture is they lumped feelings and emotions together and tried to have neither and it has produced anger so they need to take back feelings not emotions. That is why we say males in our culture think with their penis because it seemed that that was ok to feel with that part of their body. It is more in the understanding of emotions than the experience that is needed. In psychology we talk about flat effect as a problem so that makes us afraid that not to show emotions is wrong. When I say, "You just ticked me off" and I show no anger, it is feared that you will not take me seriously, and culturally that maybe true but that is a big problem today in our culture as we are so accustomed to emotions as a indicator for action. So no emotional affect is good. Now excitement is ok all the time as they are feelings. Go ahead and say excitement are emotions but the thoughts behind it are feelings.

Feelings are said to be the language of the soul. spirit, energy or essence. So why does God not feel our pain? He understands it but not feel it for that part of behavior are learned. It is not spirit but flesh and a good reason for finding a separation in them. When you learn not to have emotions in a situation but can remain concerned you have the experience of feelings without emotions. This is clear thought. We have all had glimpses of this when we are not invested in the outcome of a situation.

My son asked if you ever just get to a point where you are tired of life? Not suicidal but just a desire to go home. Some of us know home more than others. Yes, is the answer to his question but I believe this is where you are ready to let go and let God, Spirit or the Universe direct more of your life. This is more of a mind set or thought than a behavior. A very important thought.

I believe one is ready to start a new phase in their life which is one of freedom. Free to be me and uncover what is within and created by God in you rather than what you created by going to school or in other educations and etc. You are less concerned about outcome and more into the process of the situation, event or thing. Things can mean others as we are ready to go inside. It is all inside, everything you need. God/"It" is within also you get in touch with gut/intuition or that still small voice. The more you use these mediums the more they increase. Practice, practice and practice.

Less care about outcome does not mean we care less it means we stop trying to put round pegs in square holes or vise versa. We let things take their course and with some excitement for outcome. We are more into the process rather than outcome or our directing it's going. Ilis makes life have more freedom and can be fun. This is where I drive others nuts and I am ok with not knowing where it is going. We can be aware more of things not expected and the fit is better than we ever dreamed. This does take us out of our comfort zone and can be scary. Perfect timing and perfect fit. The unexpected is always amazing and a new awareness. God gives us the desires of our heart in his way; amazing. "It" really does know what "It" is doing!

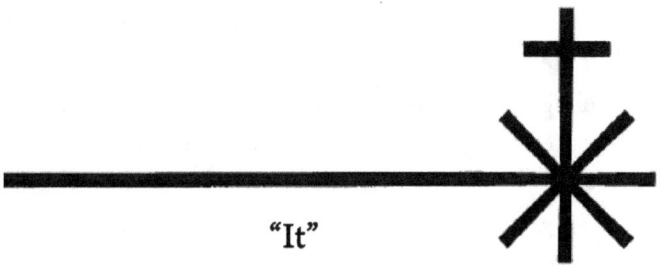

"It"

It cannot be said enough that we have made God in the image of man. How can God be human and why should we want "It" to be human in today's age. This is the stumbling block for many and a reason for the decline in church goers. First "It" is neither female or male. are human roles or traits. "It" is not Father to us all but part of us all. If we were there in the beginning of time and creation, and we were, we were all part of what? Certainly not in human form and this should delight our soul, spirit, essence and etc. as being part of the whole makes a lot of sense in explaining many of our teachings in the religions of the world. All religion were bases in love, man distorted that Great Love. That image of self and God. That part of being "part of it all". In seeing ourselves as part of the all our choices would be thought out better. Try to visualize being part of the event or present in creation, then part of the whole and that you still are. Each and everyone is important in the whole of it all. Maybe now it will be easier to see that we are all one. What happens to one happens to all, even God. It does not affect "It" as it does humans but it touches God as that is within.

Here are more current events that might help us see this concept of we are all one. Look at the recent events like the shootings at schools.; Did you know how it affected you? Do you take any responsibly for it happening? You likely say "No". But you are! Do not through the book at me as we do not want to think we are. It happened way off there Remember Christ saying that "if we do it to one we do it to all "Did you reach out to someone who feels no one cares, no one is lessening and there is no one there to look up to anymore, and no one knows the truth.

They are not as mentally ill as we want to brush them off as. Why do we want to excuse it as mentally ill people? Well it takes it out of play for us. We are off the hook. But are we? NO! So I take responsibility for these people feeling the way they do and resorting to such angry acts. That is what they are is angry not mentally ill. Males in our culture are very angry. We are the most violent society in the world. I also want to say blind as we go about doing nothing to reach out and embrace our different ness. We make laws that are not the answer as we can now see things are getting worst as laws take responsibility away from all of us. Why do I say we are a Totalitarian society. Too many laws and governed by few. Another good example of confusing law is the move over law as I traveled some 6,000 miles this year and watched the confusion and near accidents it nearly caused. Most of us when could were already doing it. Tractor trailer seem to be the most confused as they sit up high in their cabs and see before the cars what is happening so get over right in front of cars that are not ready as they do not yet know the full picture.

Just change your thinking and concepts for that is all it takes to see "It" in a more useful and realistic way since she/he is in everything and is everything. there is no excuse for being ignorant today as there is evidence all around us to the truth. Nature is the most common evidence. Look at a tree and see it having eternal life. You say oh no it does not I cut it down and burn it. It still has life in ashes. It just took on a different form and the ashes became fertilizer for my garden. Food for plants became food for me and the food for me became energy for me to plant another tree or care for a tree. Everything can be reduced to energy which was there in the beginning and will always be, just in different forms. This is the cycle of life and as well as it's mystery.

You never know where something is going to end up, for I am remodeling a home built in 1925, that was nearly destroyed by Katrina and some of the old wood I am reusing, and it looks new on one side. The side that looks new was protected from wear and tear and painting. That tree is still living in a different form. You die, take on new forms and have eternal life. There is a spirit or energy of a tree. Hug a tree and feel the energy of it. Study the symbolic uses of trees in the Bible. The tree of life. You are the branches and I am the vines. Visualize again being part of "It" for this is important for growth as you see yourself as part of each experience you have. Each experience is not happening in a vacuum. Stop seeing them apart from you and see them there for a good reason. Good business practices help workers see themselves as part of the product being produced. This is what life should be also as we see ourselves in each experience we have as a chance to grow and learn from the experiences.

My son just had a job experience that was astounding as they used intimation as a technique to get workers to produce. He lasted three months as it was not his style of ethics and they claimed to be a Christian company. He had no desire to become what they were. I had a lot of fun with this experience as I saw them as creeping on all fours Christians, as in hands and knees. This is an observation rather than a judgment. Intimation is fear based and "It" is love based. Fear would keep the employee's from feeling part of the produce. Just not a good way to treat fellow human beings. or anything as a matter of fact. You bring to you what you fear. A good reason to get rid of our fears. So if you need to intimate, you fear the lack of production or profits, than you will likely get just that in the long run. What goes around does come around unless you change the way you think.

Many religions are fear based some more than others. "It"/God is very needy in this fear based belief when he basically needs nothing from us. Again, why would a creator of everything need anything? We learned that God is Omni which means the all and everything. Case closed!

"Everything is energy or it is nothing", said Einstein. This fact makes your thoughts energy and why it is said that your prayers are answered before you ask. Because thoughts come before speaking. I always said that I was glad no one could read my mind but now I know that God/"It" can. No real comfort there. It is like having God in the bedroom. Like it or not "It" is!!

God is neither female or male but both. Androgynous is a term used for both female/male. If we are to become more God like than we should desire to be androgynous. Now that is not about our anatomy but about our thinking. It would help if you would at this point take a look at how you see yourself in this area, example where are you when it comes to certain tasks? Do you think that is a females job or males job in regard to tasks? History has proven itself wrong in so many of these areas over the past 50 years. We still in our culture have not a female president which is about to change. Time is right so Hillary is a shoe in.

If we were told we could not do this or that we may have not tried. Culture has had a long history of separating tasks. There were always those who broke the norms of the days but being alone was not comfortable or it was that being different was fun. I majored in math my teacher was female and we were supposed to believe that women could not do math. That always floored me.

We are all responsible for what we believe or think so no excuses if you are stuck in old cultural thinking.

Many people blame God for their beliefs when in reality love would never look like that idea. So a good question to ask yourself in a belief is," What does love look like?" When changing our beliefs there is a struggle internally with the old belief and the new which is natural but just part of the process of letting go of the idea that has maybe worked for you for some time. Some people say this is hard for it looked like the truth and it was for a time You were not wrong in your old belief, you did not have or was not ready for the new concept as you lacked information that was needed to change the old beliefs. If you have new information that changes your belief; it is growth and that is how it works. It is not about wrong or right.

What you knew yesterday was for yesterday. The saying is when I was a child, I believed and behaved as a child, now I have put childish ways behind me. I was not wrong as a child. I just was. We have phases and beliefs that we go through. Our competitive society keeps us in a wrong/ right mode. There is no wrong or right. Ponder that for awhile as it is likely a change in your belief. It's like good/bad, there is neither. It is all in the prospective.

In real truth your beliefs should be changing all the time or you are not growing. Now grow only if you want too as there is no right or wrong. You are, however, what you believe. It does define you. You are also not growing if you do not own your beliefs but they are what you were told and you believed them. Being told does not make them truths. as you must test and try them to see. God did say test and try me. Boy, I have done that. Authority does not always end up being good authority. Try too may not know all the facts, as they are being expounded upon all the time. I believe the Bible was a big influence in my thinking as well as math. Testing your beliefs are not encouraged in our culture so this is foreign to many. Look our teaching in schools today are a mess, as we want cookie cutter kids and make no allowance for difference in a healthy way. Oh we have programs but they come at the cost of being less than rather than equal too. It is much easier to be led. today than to think for oneself. It is just so much easier to accept something as truth than to investigate it for truth. With so much information at our finger tips there is no excuse for not exploring concepts.

If God said so then God owns that belief until you test and try it for yourself. Am I out on a limb? No!

God gave me that idea.

Now to own an idea you must reason out, why you (YOU) think it has some truth to it because the authority for you is you. It ends up being your truth, the only truth that has or should have value for you.

It is all energy and thinking is the powerhouse.

It is harder for the older generation, which I am, to change old beliefs and I have been told by them that they like it, like it is. They have little desire to be out there on that limb by themselves. Some have gotten very comfortable with the beliefs that got them thru this far and do not care to learn. I do have a very dear friend who is 99 and still open to some new ideas and reads three newspaper a day. Sharp fascinating guy.

Why is he fascinating? He always has current events to talk about and an opinion.

I believe the reason most elderly do not understand the need to continue to grow is because they were not told that life is a continuous journey and what eternal life really is all about. We are a produce of our times and if it worked for you why change it?

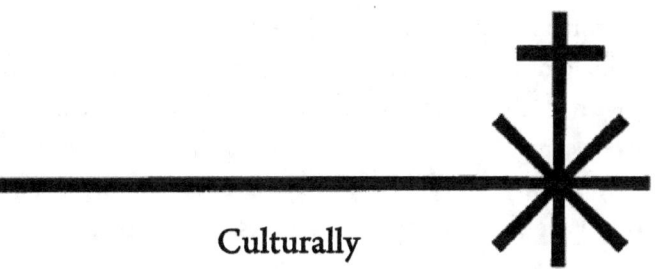

Culturally

Continuous journey is my argument for limiting our senators and representatives in congress as some are just ego and behind the times. I do believe this makes our culture move so slowly as many want us to just follow and be lead rather than free thinkers. Common core ideas! The bigger issue is control and power over. Political leaders want us to just believe that they have us and our best interest in mind. Why is Trump popular? He is crazy but it is better than what we have had from the Republican party The youth and party lever voters like him no matter how damaging he is to our imagine around the world. All because it is a change and the same old is just not cutting it. To youth he is a breath of fresh air. Talk about exposing us as ego he is doing a good job.

The last people that are going to understand what just happened is the Republican party. Pure human behavior exposed.

Ego is self-interest not other's interest in mind. It is our mask we wear until we dig deep within to the authentic self. Our journey is to help us get rid of ego. frees us to be oneself and not driven by power or control. This is the way you really get to know God/"It". It is awesome, not a chore at all but a lot of hard work. Buddha did not give up wealth and comfort and sit under the tree without a lot of sacrifice.

Wars are all about power and control. Now you may not like ALL in this statement but I do because civilized peoples do not war. So what do they do? My Bible tells me to go to my brother/sister and negotiate. If that does not work than go to a mediator or higher-level negotiator. If that does not work pray about it with all present leaving it with a higher power which is clever as by that time it gives all those involved time to cool off. Do not say it will never work for in many cases it already has. I know we have the United Nations etc. but we have not laid out this plan for all to be a part of and the USA is likely the biggest stumbling block. Love my country but I am not blind to its short comings. This is dictated to work. Whether you are in a partnership, company, or world affairs negotiation this is something you do in maturity. learn to do. Now the United States is adolescence at its best. We are still in that win/lose phase. If we would not be so invested in outcome It takes time and reworking till all can live with the solution. Civilized societies do this but we call them backward. Yet, we can see how war causes death to the incident, destruction, more enemies, anger, it is costly where a few gain and no one really wins. It only ensures another war in the future as there is no growth in war, just muscle. So until we see that war is not the way to go we will see it as the answer to debuts. %ere is more citizens speaking out about stopping wars. A Women president in the US would help but she will have it tough with the male ego and mopping up after them.

At this time in our history we have very little common sense It has been lacking for a long time and taken us to a very bad time but that can also be the good news as with the major unrest in our country we will have to find basic solutions and wisdom in the solutions. Standard anything is bound to be a problem as we see in education and common core. We are and intended to be different and not cookie cutter beings. Another example of no common sense is too many laws. Studies have shown for years that they cause lawlessness and not deter what it was intended to curtail. It also takes decision making away from those it would protect and produces complacency.

Authorities

If this goes back to what you believe. You can see that the so-called authorities are not necessarily authorities. They reinvent the wheel and do not accomplish what is intended. we need more input from the masses and youth. Youth many times have more common sense than not. If adults would respect and listen to youth, we could grow faster. This is one reason for the unrest in youth in our society. One thing I learned in my raising my children is that they taught me more than I taught them. This is only possible if you are paying attention.

As women come into politics more things will change and has changed our society. God made female/male for a balance. Women are known for more common sense and less need for power over. Equality is more important than not because common sense dictates the need for the balance. Men will not give up the power or throne voluntarily but it is happening today and long overdue. The right thing happening for the wrong reason. Women are finally ready too as unrest is the real reason for the change. Women did like being taken care off for too long or we would have rebelled some time ago. Standing up and being heard as well as voting is important. Your vote does count. If you do not vote then you have forfeited your right to complain when things go wrong.

This transitional phase is a real struggle for both female and males Women need to remain feminine and not try to emulate the male as that defeats the purpose for change. They are struggling with power and control issues as they learn to balance the two. The common-sense approach is needed not that any one person has the answers for all. Again look at the Japanese way of making everyone a part of the product in management. Males need to step back and realize that they do not lose anything if they do not have the answer for the masses. The days for thinking you know it all have gone as life is a lot more complicated today. The less laws the less we will get stuck in old drama or dogma. One size does not fit all or for all times. Sensitivity is so needed and not a bad thing. A gentle touch is needed and no one powering over.

We need the female/male balance which I know was intended by God for even "It" does not power over you. "It" is unconditional love. No need to separate gender at all. Be more androgynous. Get rid of ego which I believe is proof of androgynies or God like. Not a bad goal to seek. Pure unconditional love. Since love is all there is. Think of it, if I had no need for preference than I would chose always in fairness and love. No personal gain needed or wanted.

Remember the story of the two women who claimed to be the mother of a child in King Solomon days?

Well he said we will have to cut the child in two and you can both have half. He knew that the real Mom would give up the child. Common sense or wisdom, one and the same. It is hard to be common sense when you have non pure motives. One of the biggest flaws in politics today is the policy in having to follow party lines. It has lead our country down the wrong roads. It makes our decision making come with a return expected and not of an impartial motive. Payoffs have just gotten out of hand along with riders to important bills. In the short term someone benefits but in the long term no one does as it perpetuates the practice. Another reason for my saying we do not have a democracy. Change does not happen willingly in our individual lives or culturally. Not many gives up what they worship, money, fame, self, youth, power and control voluntarily. They usually are forced by circumstances. That is a shame as it is better to go to the water willingly than be forced into it. We lack foresight and if we see it coming we turn a blind eye hoping it will go away. The bully and the young teenager as adolescence, which our country is at the present time in growth and development. Women will make the transition to community and make for a balance, hopefully.

"It" Is God

The real meaning of life is to become all you can become and it is a never-ending journey from one life time to another and eternity. The getting rid of ego and personal gain in everything is part of it all.

It will take the balance of female/male to balance the power and control that has taken us to an ugly place here in the US and abroad. For our image abroad is a laughing matter but they cannot afford to cause us anger as they see us sink. Just keep printing the old mighty dollar until it is more and more worthless. I had this conservation in 1991 or 92 in Germany, so you see we still don't get it. Change is so slow by itself but tragedy will force it to happen. Our next big tragedy will be our economics. Basically we are pompous fools. Fooling ourselves. This is not a judgment but an observation.

In the 1960's we made fun of the "flower children" and back to earth people who had a good point to make but the powers to be were not ready to get the message. They were the churches and governing bodies Most of the common population was not either. People who do see these disasters coming do nothing for fear of losing what they have when in fact they will sooner than later. Why do those who see bullying not do anything about it? For fear of being the next one to be bullied. See what a self-centered population we are? ADOLESENCE. Fear is adolescence and is. used in our culture to keep people in line. Fear is the opposite of love. We have had many chances to move ahead in our culture but it was squashed by powers to be. The 1970's had a very tragic event, the Kent State massacre. This tragedy was our Tentiman Square. Like we ignore the voice of youth we use to rely on the college kids to help us go in the right direction. Have you noticed that they are silent now. We do not even have a Jane Fonda standing up for good change.

In the Bush administration in the 1990's fear was used in the most blatant way as it was pared with patriotism Fear of speaking out left everyone confused and paranoid. Fear in the hearts of the citizens left the government freewheeling that is our downfall and the worst is yet to come as we have not tried to turn ourselves around. See how easy it is to get off track in doing the right thing? All for power over and control.

Are we a democracy when control is in the hands of the few? We are a totalitarian government, a government of few and too many laws. Democracy is for the people by the people and of the people. Yes we have a voting system but it is not one vote covers all and it so costly that the likely good guys cannot afford to run for office. Democracy is for the masses not the few. Most citizens of the US do not even know the driving force behind the economics in our country.

If you are having a hard time believing these ideas, just take a moment and take a look at the attacks that each party and their attacks on each other for power and control. They care not for truth or fact but winning and attention. Look at the Obama birth place or Cruz's. Even when truth is shown some are really not wanting the truth. Why? Ulterior motives and we believe what we want to believe and justify it by where it came from. There are those who still believe in authority as having the truth and are looking out for our best interest. How many took the time to realize that the media is not the authority on much, when they heard a prominent news reporter embellish on a story and get caught. How many times does this happen? We should be angry about the deception by our politicians, media or industry. We have strayed from the path of creditability and it started with even the churches who for power and control of the masses lied about much. Do you know that churches are faithful to their domination not you.? We all say we do not have time to check out the truth as just making ends meet leaves us exhausted. Did you ever hear that is what our government want from us so we do not question for the truth. We are insulted by our government and churches as they tell us we could not understand the truth so they must protect us from ourselves. To know the truth will set you free. Youth are more aware of these truths and it is a good source of their anger. We are a very angry society and ready to explode at a moment. Young adults who came into therapy with me would tell it like it was and I would have to tell them that they were seeing it just like it was but they needed to focus on their education and try to make it a better world. I love the youth that tell it like it is but struggle with what to do with it because they are still incident enough to be thinkers. Education can certainly squash that.

Give us enough rope and we will hang ourselves> That really means that we get the opposite we want out of a it for our endeavors. Maybe what goes around comes around and backfires!

Now why all the negativity? It all goes back to thinking. Thinking the powerhouse. You are what you believe. Start now to take responsibility for your beliefs. Check the history of your beliefs. It is really an eye opener for a lot of the background for your beliefs are motivated by power and control. Economics being the bottom line.

So how do we get back some of our basic values? Well, first by speaking out about what is not ringing true for you. You are your authority. You take that to your grave as it is thought. We need to move to community and away from adolescence. The rich only get rich off you and your retirement. You have a lot of power there so decide not to worry about tomorrow and let tomorrow take care of itself. Bible says that. Many people found out that their savings go down when the stock market goes down; they learned during the ;08 recession. But you still see the media talking about savings. Savings are probably safer under your pillow now than any place else. So middle class you have a lot of power in your savings which might be more secure if you invest in your community. There are rumors of back to local or buy in your community and that is a starting place. To fight a allergic reaction to pollen in your area you should buy honey from your area. Take that principal further and develop a habit of being aware of where something is coming from. We have had outbreaks of food contaminations that should be an eye openers. In your flower garden place some vegetables like lettuce or cabbage.

Adolescence's soon find out that they are not the center of the universe and that they need the others. So for us we need each other. What happens to one happens to all. The self has to be healthy or on its way to bring healthy in order to see this need for community. Think of being on a deserted island and accomplishing something and having no one to share it with. The success of it is short lived.

Treasure Island by Robert L Stevenson was about moving from self and being ready for the others or community. Friday came when Robert had processed the self and was ready to share his life with another. Lot more fun. Self is very important but our culture does not do a very good job in this area so we are still in adolescence. When you are ready for community there is a joy and contentment in it all, not a loss of self. but an addition to self. A new phase to life. Culturally there is no institution that does a good job in this phase for they are in adolescence also. Most psychiatry is useless as it is just take this pill and you will feel better. Of course you do for a while but the issues are still there and a pill is not the answer as it is for the symptoms and not the cause of the problem. Thinking is the powerhouse. If it is a chemical imbalance than you still need to change the way you look at the issues or problems in the situation. Cause and effect are part of nature and Gods natural laws. Causes will not go away on their own and you do not have to learn from them if you do not want too. Did you ever watch Two and A Half men? That psychiatrist did nothing for Charlie on TV or in real life. Now that may not be fair to the good well-meaning psychiatrists but the point is that masking the symptoms is just that. Causes are deep within and that is where you must go. We are all very insecure, always or at times. That is what adolescence is all about.

We have been duped into believing there is security. Defining security as safe, confident, free and protected can help you see there is no such thing. Yet we use the word as if it means all these things.

Free from uncertainty - no such thing. Free form the hazards of losing no way. Eat healthy exercise and have a good attitude and you will have a long prosperous life = no way. We have seen people who have done and believe all these things and still leave planet earth young. You bring to you what you fear so fear nothing and you will have a less stressful life and peaceful life. Peace is more likely what can be securely found in life.

To be God like is to need nothing, fear nothing and want nothing beyond your means. God/ "It" needs nothing from you. You would not have free will if "It" did. Because we are an economic based society, we are always in need so it is hard to think that everyone or things are not like us always in the want stage. This is taught so it is not a have to have. No group or institution in the US culture teaches you what is truly needed for a good free life because everything is about economics and it is the driving force. This driving force causes us to not see or hear what the real issues in our society are so we can move beyond it. Like the 60's had a good message but it was squashed and made fun of. How many crashes do you need in your savings or retirement to understand where your money goes? We are all gamblers in the stock market. Who makes the money? Madoff was his own stock market. We condemn him for stealing from others. I believe the good life is too simple for it to be believed.

Now I have had a good life without any security or money except enough. Never knew what a savings really was and did not have fears or anxiety over it. It likely came from my dad as I remember asking him, "what would he do with a million dollars?" and he said, "give it to some poor devil who needed it worse than he did". Now that was from the heart and Dad was a very happy man who really had nothing as I would say he never had two dimes to rub together. But I know today that when I wanted a dollar to go with my friends to a dance, he likely gave me his last dollar to go because he wanted to see me happy. Now I baby sat or clean homes for .50 cents a day so I could go roller skating or to a dance as it cost one dollar to get in. were the good days. You struggled but it was just part of life.

Tolerance is not one of our culture's strong points. Our economy would not like us to all going back to the earth for the middle class really fuels the country. Hey, middle class you have a lot of power and all you have to do is ban together. Does that sound like community? What would the driving force be if not money? It would be tolerance for differences and joy in others joy. It would be God like finding the joy in our joy. "It" intended us to be different or "It" would have made us alike. That simple. We must first love ourselves as created. Differences should be seen as beauty. I encourage you to recreate yourself a new each day and become all you can be. Think out of your own box. "It" would be a lot more fun as the same old is boring after a while. Remember your soul leaves your body especially at night to go home to regenerate as you are stuck and spirit so to speak cannot interfere with your progress very much. Being unhappy should be seen as progress instead of something to run away from. We grow faster in our unhappiness as we search for answers. If we are very predictable, we are heard less often and that is why the adolescence hears us less. Why is it that the ones closest to us see the change in us last? They have become used to your predictability and fail to see the change. Have you ever said, "but I do not do that anymore". We think that steadfastness is the way to go but it might indicate just a comfort zone and a fear of change and growth. Some growth will happen whether you are conscientious of it or not but it is better to be aware of growth as it will bring joy to your life. This is high on life experiences and being aware is the key. It is like practice. practice or like attracts like and energy attracts more energy. Feeling accomplished is a joy in life. Charge your battery by being aware of life. There are two kinds of people in the world; the living and the walking dead. The living are aware and the walking dead are just going thru the motions of life. Who do you want to be? What do you want to be? Those questions should be taught to us young. One of the lasting and most painful experiences in my young life was when my Dad told me he was disappointed in my behavior. That is a powerful technique in parenting. It told me I was responsible for my behavior and that I needed to be aware.

Churches and schools do not help us to think for ourselves as they dictate to us what to believe. College is a little better but a little to much useless history, teach it but do not test on it. Obama just stated that schools needed to be less about testing and more about teaching. I believe he means students should have more encouragement with flexibility, like debates, and discussion groups and with out of the box ideas.

Over the years God and I have had many debates with no win/loss feelings. I used to drive several hours by myself and when I did I visualized God as my passenger and would say, "Well God what are we going to discuss today as I have a nine hour drive". I had wonderful revelations during these talks and before you comment- they were real I will tell you one that happened on a shorter trip coming home from my Mom's.

I heard, "If Jesus comes again what will it be called?" I said, "His second coming." I knew just what was being asked by God's statement. I was being a brat mainly because a time ago I had been confronted with reincarnation and had asked if we could put it on the shelf for awhile and that request was honored. Now was the time and I knew it. So that still small voice quietly stated again, "If Jesus comes again what will it be called?" This time I answered, "The reincarnated Jesus". It was such an awesome experience that I nearly had to pull over as the tears started to flow. You see I had to study hypnosis in order to help than called multiple personality disorder and ran into past lives regression therapy and was not ready for it so asked to put it on the shelf. God does not give you what you cannot handle. The Bible says," that my sheep will know my voice and we are all God's sheep according to the analogy.

So what is God rather than who is God?

God, "It", Spirit, Soul, Ali are one and the same and are formless. No need to bring them down to human levels or forms. Everything is energy which is formless. Your thoughts are energy in a flash. In our awareness we know them to be formless and can become comfortable in the formlessness. Now we have debated for years whether the voice is inside or outside and for me it is so auditable but I believe it is within since everything I need is within. It does not matter as it does not change anything and are the mysteries of the Universe and the beauty of being formless. The process in human growth is awareness, enlightenment, and advancing the already beliefs you have. What you know will always need some adding too. I think we have the idea that once learned that is the end and it is not as we live in an ever-changing world of seeing and believing.

You can only manifest what you know or believe or when you are ready to let go of old knowledge and move to a higher level of reasoning. A good example is being stuck in teachings of 2000 plus years ago for God is with us in this 21st century. This makes the teachings history only and not that helpful for the modern day plus like anything repeated over time it is not really taken to heart anymore. What Jesus taught was sound teaching but remember he came to change some teachings that were not true. He came to change the world not keep it static. Stay where you are if you like as there is no wrong/right but realize he said greater things you will do than this and we are not seeing that for the most part. Many are called but few are chosen as we are not willing. I believe Jesus must be very disappointed in us as we have been astray or stuck What Jesus said is what is important not who he was. Control and power was what corrupted the system of his day and we can see it is still operating strongly today. We must think for ourselves in order to have a personal relationship with God or even know God Institutions are not teaching free thinking as much as just memorizing and spiel it back in a test. Fear is a factor as we want that degree so again do not speak out. Back to school and needing more discussion groups and debates in class rooms. This teaches that it is ok to have a different idea about something and strengthens character. The teachers are not the problem, it is that their hands are tied by the states or government and all about the test scores.

So what stops us from speaking out is fear of being ridiculed, scorned, made fun of, unsupported and mostly being alone in our beliefs. Say, wasn't Jesus feeling all these things? In my belief, Jesus was human as a highly evolved being so I am sure he felt alone so went off to be by himself to get grounded again as it is not easy to be alone in our beliefs.

Jesus knew likely all the religions of the world at the time as he was about his Fathers work and Buddhism was wide spread. Now Buddha taught that Buddhism was not a religion but a way of life. Jesus teachings were about a way of life. This is what is the problem with Christianity today as it is not taught as it can be applies today. Like Buddha; Jesus teachings are not practiced as a way of life. "What would Jesus do?" should be the first thought in decision making and is not used enough before acting. A so-called Christian who kills another in the defense of his or her beliefs is acting out anger not as a Christ follower.

I love the thought of my faith being a way of life because it is then not static but an ever-evolving process. Being open each day to new understanding is important as there is no need to be on planet earth if it isn't to experience and grow. Some people on their death bed learn the true meaning of life. Why wait until then!

Life is a process of becoming and getting rid of ego. If ego is processed and left behind than free thinking and speaking your truth is easier. Who knows maybe your truth could change the world. All fears are based in ego. We are all in the process of becoming whether we are aware or not.

Some go willing to the water and some are pushed in. There is no fear speaking out as it can be fun like in a debate. Play devils advocate so to help develop new ways of seeing something as it is all in the perspective. So what if no one agrees with you at the time, just go on with the idea or thought if it seems to have some draw for you. Over the years I have had these experiences only to have my beliefs become common knowledge. %ink out of the box. This is a great test for ego.

It is not about the others it is about peeling away the layers to find the true self. What you were given and what you can become with what you were born with as potential. You lack nothing. Do not look to others to define you. Know yourself. It is surprising how many people never give a thought to who or what they are.

I ran a panic disorder group for nine years and panic attacks are caused by your fears. Fear of not being enough, not measuring up, and the death and dying issues. Life is eternal so there is no death and when you really believe that than fears can go away. In death we just change forms and go back to where we came, back to the whole. Nothing to fear but fear itself so take the fear out of death. Take the sting out of fear and death.

As long as you keep God human or with human traits, you will likely stay stuck in old teachings. As you get rid of ego and become more God like; death and life make more sense. Since God did not die and is giving as many revelations as "It" always did to those who will listen Everything is moving along with everything else. You should want to keep learning, remembering and growing. Your soul knows why it doesn't just hit us upside the head and clue us in. Because discovery is an important part of our journey and the joy of God and life. Free will is an important key. It makes for less wrong/right issues as we will get to where we are going sooner or later and learn or remember much in the process. Remember Jesus getting angry at the followers for wanting more and more miracles? The reason was that in miracles you miss steps necessary for ownership of the process. There are no miracles, just the lack of explanation which is not known yet. There is nothing new in the universe, just things to discover. There is the reason for discovering self. What else is in me that I am not aware of? Potential!!! Uncover potential. We fear the unknown and are a primary reason for fearing change. One miracle is all that is needed to know there is much mystery in life to discover. That is the good news. Many people do not want to know as the like it the way it is. This boggles my mind but life is not what it seems to be. We can get comfortable as creatures of habit but that is likely stopping growth.

Here is one issue that boggles my mind as I watch all those running in races for cancer with no knowledge that there have been many cures for cancer that got squashed by institutions, government, and associations that benefit from the big industry and business of health and medicine. Drug firms real a lot of power and control. Read Daniel Haley's book, "Politics In Healing". It is a well-documented cures and what happen to them. The book infuriated me and I went to see Dan before he died in his nursing home. The use of force and money will shake your naive world as it did mine. Now I do believe most providers start out wanting to help but get caught up in the politics of their careers and go astray. Clean up some of our organizations that benefit from our being sick in our culture. Tie US uses more drug than any other culture. I am what I call a 'self-healer' It is all God centered as I was told that God never intended us to be sick, so why are we? Well God also said to test and try him so I did some 40 years ago. I have not been to a doctor in 40 years and take no meds at 77 as I allow my body to heal itself. It has done a good job. FEAR is the driving force in medicine. "If you do not do this you will die". Well, what do we have to do first to overcome this fear? Deal with our beliefs in death and dying. There is no death! We have eternal life. Now my daughter died of cancer at 31 and she said that I would never get cancer because I would just say, "Whoopee, I am going home" and she was so right. "Where is thy sting oh death "Shakespeare. My dearest friend of 29 years is now 98 soon to 99 and has adopted the same attitude and wants to live to be 100. He looks like he may make it unless he decides it is no longer his goal. It is up to him not God. Thank you, God, for that knowledge. My friend and I do not let fear drive our health. If God gives us the choice to live or die why is man not? First you have to believe that God gives us a choice Your choice may be as simple as not taking care of yourself in eating, drinking, exercise, attitude or any unconscious death wish. We are all committing suicide one way or another in neglecting what would help keep us healthier. Seeing free will is deeper than you thought. My friend understands when I say I do not want to live to be one hundred as he knows my drive and reason for life this time around.

As you quest for the truth, you do find it. Many give up because they do not trust themselves to find it or are not worthy of getting the answers or rely on what they already know as it was told to them. Who is your authority? Self! Knock and you will find, ask any you will receive. Put that to the test. Like I did when I got in the car for a trip and asked God what are we going to talk about? Who would have thought that my life would have involved driving long distances and my revelations would come in that way. So test and try God to find a quiet time for you. No way does it have to be boring or in a vacuum. You can be snow blowing, gardening, mowing lawns, or anything that is not taking away from a task. We are unique and important individuals and one size does not fit all. Again we are already given all we need to do our unique journey. Now it may not be president of anything but it is a part that is important. Part of the whole. It has been my pleasure to study and read all my life to find the answers to the truth in many fields but a dedication too. We look to pleasure for the answers to a good life but I can tell you that if you are doing what will further your knowing of anything it will be a pleasure. Knowledge is thought and that which you take with you when you go home to spirit world. This writing is fun (now do not let my friends know this as they heard me say I did not want to do any more writing as I was not a writer) What you are given, you give away or it has no lasting value. It will always have value to me but sheer pleasure to give it away. I already know that everyone cannot embrace some of these ideas and we are slow to change as most Americans do not like change. But I am a human behaviorist and have had years of experience in people changing and loving the change.

Family Structure

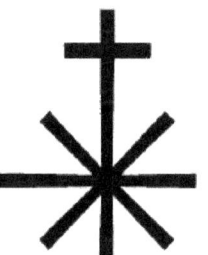

Were you told to just go along with things that you wanted to challenge when you were a kid? I was and my biggest fear to overcome was being different but thank goodness coming from a big family they taught me it was ok to be different. At a young age I became an overachiever as I was a middle child and had to find some way to stand out and get noticed or be happy with being ignored. Now this standing out is not done on the conscious level but the unconscious level. I first chose to excel in school and become a perfectionist. I was a perfectionist because it is something one needs to modify as you see it isn't working for you as you get older. I call it in remission now for the most part. All my life I feel I have had strong support from my parents and the spiritual. I say spiritual as in farming life it takes several guardian angels to protect us. Me from myself as I loved to learn and was very physically active. We did some dare devil thing as we had creative minds and tested the limits sometimes with no fears. I was 7 when my parents bought the farm and it was a good life and it shaped my life.

It was at this time that I was knowingly leaving my body each night to go to spirit world. This is very vivid today as it was then. I would create as vortex and go through it to a spirit world. The purpose I believe was to keep me strong on the unconscious level for my life ahead. It was never an easy life but a very creative one. It is true that you choose your script for life but free will also plays a role and I can tell you where my free will played out. Not every detail is scripted. My daughter liked the books that you could choose several different ways to read them and that is more like real life as you can choose many different ways to learn

"It" Is God

the same experience in life so to grow and learn or remember. Life is about you!! Your experiences are your teachers. Being conscious about what the experience is teaching you will help you process much faster and it should not be so laboring and let you in on what some of the issues are in your life. Discomfort is usually a key to the teaching of the experience. We like to put discomfort behind us as fast as we can but that should not be the case. That is why it is important to have others in your life to share your thoughts with. Many time the others are not going to help much but that is when you know that they are not your answer. It is one of those dichotomies in life, when to and when not too. When I was a kid and no one was talking about it, whatever it was, then I knew that it was mine to ponder. As you move closer to being more God like and let go of ego- you begin to understand more of your life and it's remembering as opposed to culturally learning's. One of the mysteries for me in my leaving my body at night as a 7- and 8-year-old since no one seemed to talk about it, how did I know to do it.? Where did it come from as an idea? Interesting? Well I still do not have the answers to it all but It shaped my life as the spiritual quest was never far from my thoughts and the mysteries of life are so fascinating. I like Shakespeare as he wrote about life and its mysteries with quotes of there is more to life than meets the eye. Paying attention to those things in life that you are always drawn to will help you find some of the purposes of your life this time around. We are not left in the dark as much as we have been led to believe, we have just not had good teachers. These teachers do not likely have the answers so cannot give them to you. Maybe a good part of the design as to discover something is to know something for itself. Otherwise it is told to you and not your discovery. My reading some 50 books a year, praying continuously, and a positive attitude paid off. Along with looking for the revelations in my life. Sounds like too much work. Well it can also be my favorite word, "fun". How so? Human beings are about change so the discoveries of a new concept, ideas or truths can make you high on life. High on life is no small matter as I am still in awe when these things happen; new concepts, ideas, or truths. To live really live you must set sometime to ponder what you are experiencing. This is why prayer without seizing is part of a spiritual life. To zone out is fun and yes you may have to turn off TV, get away from your cell, and etc. but the joy received from doing so will be rewarding. I have been accused of being in my head too much but let me tell you what you take with you when you go home to spirit world is thoughts and it makes a big difference What would be your ideal thought that you would like to have just the second before you die?? That is how important it is so decide and practice, practice and practice. If life is eternal and it is than you just go on in the mode you were in upon death. That should scare a lot of us. Death should not be feared so take the sting out of it by making it joy. Nothing to do with leaving before you are ready but in the right timing. Use words like, going home, going back, going to be with God, or to heaven and yes if you must to a better place. No such thing as a better place but well-meaning people say it all the time as they fear saying anything too spiritual. Using positive phases is a good place to start to take the sting out of death and will help to cross over to spirit world upon death. Emotional traits fall away upon death but feelings do not. Remember feelings are the language of the soul. Feelings are directed by thoughts.

Emotions

Being objective as much as possible, takes the emotion out of play. When we say that we like our drama it refers to becoming accustomed to our emotions. They are maybe exciting but can lead you astray and many times away from the truth in a situation. Our emotions are subjective meaning they are part of the false self and ego. So letting go of ego will help you be more objective. We have a better chance of doing the right thing for the right reason. %inking the powerhouse and is energy. Objectiveness is an advantage as it is in the present moment, not in the past or future experiences. You are judging the decision from the moment. It can be called a pure response which is God. You will know God/ "It" in the pure response. It is joyful. The Bible and Buddhism taught the present moment ideas. Peter, trying to walk on water until he reflexes on what he was doing. with the thought of, "it cannot be" so let go of pure thought. It got contaminated with ego. The present moment is awesome and gives awesome experiences. So why fear change or challenges? It can be scary but this too shall pass. Trust! Building trust is a struggle in change and you can already know the truth but find it hard to follow as we want to follow our past experiences. To get rid of the old beliefs and stay in the now is foreign to us so is hard to believe. We have lost our creativity so do not like to venture into the unknown. A lot of our beliefs were hammered home as facts making it very hard to part with them. They were usually said with "God said so "so who could argue with God. God did not write the Bible it was maybe in part inspired. I will tell you at least half of what I once believed had nothing to do with "It"/God. They were man's need to control. Practice, practice and the news will become the new norm for you. It is an illusion to believe that we have arrived at the total truth about anything. This stops many from moving ahead; why try if it is always changing. You are not changing your beliefs as much as you are expounding upon them. Creeping precedes walking as a general rule. There was nothing wrong about creeping and it has good purposes in the childlike balance, strengths muscles and brain development. This is also as an example for processing by practice and practicing. To know something does not mean we do it. It is just head knowledge than if we practice it, we get to put it in our behavior. This may seem very elementary but this part of being or becoming is not given much thought and maybe what is missing in your process. Ever have an experience and think you got it only to experience it again down the road and you say but I already do that! Well the universe want you to make sure that you know it well and now you own it. Practice. We also see ourselves going through the experience faster and with more assurance. Remember it is someone else's idea until you make it yours. You are now the believer of the idea. In childhood we take from others our beliefs but in adulthood we take the ideas and make them ours or expound upon them or through them out. Here is another example where the masses bought into an idea in the name of God that basically had nothing to do with God and that is eating fish on Friday. It was put into the Catholic beliefs as the Italian fisherman were having a hard time making a living. It is still practiced by many. A few have knowledge of this and do not take it as anything to do with God. We have done many things in the name of God that did not have anything to do with God, like wars crusades, genocides, and so forth. God would not be on any side as we are all God's children. Unconditional love does not take sides. "It" ops for what is fair and not destructive.

"Why do I believe what I do," in adulthood is a good place to start with being open to the truth and enlightenment Some that we believe to be authorities are not necessary authorities at all. There are no authorities when it comes to God as "It" is not static but moves into what we create as it is created. Education does not stop with a piece of paper. Being open is the key to growth. We are led astray a lot more than we will know. As a Human Behaviorist I know how easy it is to cite the masses and direct the crowd. It is not difficult at all. Fear and ignorance are used for power over all the time to control the masses. We do not take responsibility for our beliefs or actions. It is easy to blame authority, the boss, the laws or others for our beliefs. There is a great need for change as there is great freedom in taking responsibility for our beliefs.

Trashing people is where the media has gone and some of those newscasters should refuse to being party to such drama, sensationalism, hype, thrills, or just plain embellishing of gossip. A recent newscaster did just that and got himself in trouble. They are so used to doing it they do not give it a second thought. It is the media's problem and the excuse is everyone is doing it. They think for some reason we want that kind of reporting. I watch TV for one hour a day if that as it adds no real dimension to my life. If I need entertainment I listen to the birds because they are cheerful and I do not feel like I need to take a bath to get rid of any negativity. I taught clients to not watch the news before going to bed as it is the first thing you process upon dreaming Have happy thought before going to bed. I like to watch Canadian news as I live on the Canadian border and it is better reporting, less sensationalism. We are a very angry society. We see this in our youth and where do they get their anger?? There is a great lack of integrity and respect at the top so our youth have little to look up too. Politicians right now seem to be at their worst as we go through these transitional periods of role changes. It should not be seen as role reversals but a balance of power. It is long overdue but never easy for those who see themselves as losing. Both sexes need to take responsibility for it taking so long for the balance of power to become a reality. Men liked being king of the roost and women liked being taken care of. To clearly see this one has to have gotten rid of a lot of ego in order to see the overall benefit for all. The other day our president talked about the transitions we are experiencing and how it is affecting politicians and our decision making. It was brilliant but he has been one of best presidents according to me! We will have to limit the length that all members of Congress can hold office to rid ourselves of politics as usual. We will also have to make it more desirable to break from party lines. These will help us be more honest and to do the right thing when making decisions for all. Women in politics will help balance the power, this just common sense and remember there is not an ounce to be found right now. There is no freedom in following party lines and who are party lines for and if it is predetermined then where is the power to do the give and take with negotiations? Why are we fed up with politics as usual? Power and control runs the system instead of what is best for all. Personal interest has taken over and limiting terms in the office will correct lot of issues we have now created. The costly elections will also be curtailed. Of course those who benefit from a broken system will fight hard as we see, to keep benefiting them. Greed and corruption are all ego. They are still at the primitive stage of win/lose. A very insecure stage of development. Some of it is not even at adolescence They feel that they are going it alone and therefore cannot be there for others. Most of our male population are still in this stage. An observation not judgment.

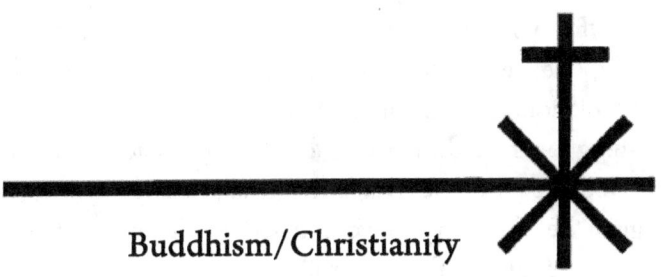

Buddhism/Christianity

In Buddhism, the way of life is to work on getting rid of ego, which consists of past and future experiences that dictate how you will respond to present situations. Buddhism says that the process is to mediate, do deep purification and empty the mind. %ese are not just in Buddhism but are in parts of Christianity, Muslimism, and many holistic approaches to health and well-being. Some feel that mediation is difficult and hard to do but it is not as there as hundreds of ways of doing it. It is not just sitting under a tree until enlightenment comes but you can do it anywhere that you get in present moment awareness. A present moment in the garden smelling the roses, going for a walk on the beach, anything that takes you out of your troubles and helps you feel them sliding away. You have done it already but just have not thought of it as mediation. It was just a magic moment when everything seemed to fall from the usual chatter in your mind. Drive a car and do not remember the last few miles, You are in a hypnotic state but more alert than when your mind is ruminating a mile a minute about something that upset you. Letting go of all that chatter is a chance for a present moment or meditative moment experience. While driving it is not something you try to do it just happened. Mediation can be that simple. Empty the mind. In Christianity it says to empty the mind to hear the still small voice; be still and know that I am God. Take in the rose while seeing its beauty.

Lost in the beauty. Change the fear of thinking that you do not know how to mediate to you already do it and it is not one way only. Just increase your awareness and do it more. In situations you will respond with clarity and present moment neutrality. Remaining neutral can only happen when you are without ego. You are not responding from past or future experiences but from present moment. Being aware is the key to your mediation. Deep purification can be summed up with doing the right thing for the right reason. So once again ego is being purified or eradicated. too is not rocket science but science never the less as you are changing the chemistry of your body by changing you thinking or behavior. Thinking of the powerhouse.

As a self-healer I believe without a doubt that we were not created to be sick. God, "It", Ali or whatever you call your higher power did not create you to be sick. God says "to test and try me "So for some 40 plus years I have done just that. This belief is part of my being. For years I have been able to be in close quarters with very sick people and not get sick.

My daughter who died at 31 because she wanted too and of cancer said that I would never get cancer as I would just say," good I am going home" and she was right My death and dying issues have been resolved -no fear- just joy but not a death wish. There is no freedom like this kind of freedom. Like the soul that has at times a struggle to stay with the body or around the body, we as human beings want more freedom. It is not a desire to die but it is one of those dichotomies in any struggle. The more positive you are about death, the sting no longer there, the easier it is to live. This alone is a good reason to deal with the negative issues around death and dying. Having more than one life time to grow and learn sure helps in a positive way. Power and control is the only reason some do not believe this or want you to. If birth is positive than so is death. Try to move toward a joy in birth and a joy in death. Again not someone else's beliefs but yours. Only you know what your beliefs and issues are and what you came to planet earth to remember or understand more fully. What makes sense to you and that will come when you go within. So go within and see what comes to mind. Dreams, repeated ideas, songs, like and dislikes all tell us something about ourselves and our journey. It is all there in your soul so bring it forth and you only need to have the desire.

"It" Is God

I am really puzzled for two mornings I have awakened with the statement of, "I Love New York" in my mind. Now this is not to my liking as I am trying to sell my home in NY and move to Mississippi at least for the winter. I even have a home in Mississippi that I felt led to buy, so what is that all about? And you say, "It is just that nothing. Why do you think it has to mean anything other than that you do love NY? Does everything happen for a reason? Culturally we blow these thing away and pay little attention to them. My life is not like that so I ponder it for a while. First, recognizing that NY is a beautiful state but just too expensive for me to live in now. I call Mississippi the best kept secret. You do not have to give each thought hours of attention but it might help your life if you slowed down some and pondered. It is a way of life for me and sometimes the thoughts go nowhere. Another dichotomy. But the message you are giving the universe is twofold, one you are ready to dig deeper in the meaning of life and two you are really ready to know yourself. and your journey. Religion never really did do much here, maybe because God was so distorted. So going inside gave you too much power and left everyone to their own personal God which was not very controllable. Controlling the masses is what is desired but even God did not intend that or "It" would have made us all alike. The difference is the beauty. It would be boring even to God if there was not free will and different chooses with different people. So you will see when going within that you feel freer and what everyone else believes is just that their beliefs and not necessarily for you. Culturally we have not been encouraged to be different. Yet at birth we are, with no finger prints alike and our ears and eyes different. Was this a mistake or left up to chance or the wonderful design. Maybe it was not the powers to be as much as our fear of being different that got us stuck. Could we help our youth more by helping them deal with the fear of being different more than helping everyone to stop bullying? Well it is easier to control the masses if we all believe the same. Now that is how power and control works. Sheep to the slaughter is a good analogy, just keep following the same beliefs just because the masses do. The most frightening example for me was during the Bush administration after 9/11. We were all lead to believe that speaking out against our government was being unpatriotic. It was followed by secrecy, wiretapping, and arrests of just people of interest. There was no balance of power or check and balance in place. Maybe most of the administration did not see what was happening at the time and we are still paying a high price for it. Most politicians at that time were not thinking for themselves as they were in office too long and just went alone rather than make waves or go against the party line. Power reeled. The 1930's are about to return in the US and deservingly so as we have no backing for our money and print it anyway. The rich go down this time as the middle class learned much during the 2008 recession. That was just the tip of the iceberg. This is not rocket science it is just common sense. The rippling effect is why it does not get fixed so what you do not take charge of on your own will eventually happen in spite of yourself. I believe in facts and common sense. The positive part of this is that it will get us back to reality. That is our lesson for the runaway politics and old farts in office that were part of the old boys society will be going down with the crash. We are all responsible for our demise. I think no one really knows what to do to fix it as it will be such a hard time and most that know hope it will correct itself which is not the natural laws of God. God is natural laws. "It" put them in place and you will abide in them. What goes around does come around as part of the natural laws of the universe. Do you see? God does not punish us we punish ourselves by bad choices and selfishness or ego. The youth in our culture see this more clearly than most adults and it drives them nuts, as they put it. The ones who are gaining from their ponzi schemes are about to punish themselves not God. They will be "blindsided" by all of this as they too are on planet earth to become and it is not rich on other people's backs. Become all they can become. You can fool some of the people some of the time but you cannot fool all of the people all of the time. The fool is the self in this case. Have you ever said, "I don't know how this happened," only to find out later that there were warning signs that you did not pay attention too. This is why if you are fully alive it is important to pay attention to what is going on in your life and less about the others. Ask questions, feel good about not knowing something as culturally we act as if we know it all. If you want to inquire about something, know nothing and watch what you get in response. My experience is if I tell what I know about whatever it is I am inquiring about, I have left the expert more confusion with where to start to tell me what I am wanting to know. Now the expert can start at the basics and give his spiel and I get more helpful information. In other words play dumb, it does not take away from your intelligence. Giving others a chance to tell you what they have learned is an act of kindness.

Since some of this seems very negative and life more complicated than you want, let me say that everything happens for a reason and it is all positive. Bad things happen to good people for a good reason. It helps us move toward freedom and that is no small feat. We do not give up our pleasures easily but with great struggles. Healthy life styles are not easy and we are always putting them off. We are in so many transitions right now, all designed due to our decisions of the past and it will likely get worse before it gets better as all transitions do. Transitions are just that and culturally most fear changes so drag their feet so it becomes more painful. There are no good old days. There is just today and what you decide to do with it. Make it different if only in the way you look at it. Thinking of the powerhouse. It is all in the perception. You can find things helpful and ponder them or know that they are not for you at this time. No right or wrong. Perception can change everything and there is really no objective ideas as the observer is always influencing the ideas. Interpretation is a key to growth and development as it is very individualized and should be. Own your perceptions and be ok if others do not believe as you do. Be unique as you intended. If something does not ring true for me, I ponder it as I know there is a missing link and that link is key to the concept. It is like a puzzle and until the last piece is in you do not have it done or the full picture. In the end of pondering I have my own take on the whatever it is that I ponder. Our perceptions are changing all the time and should be as they are in the design of things. What has happened too much of the time is that we settled for half the picture thinking that was all there was to it. To become all we can become is always changing like our bodies, the trees, animals etc.

Remember nature mimics us as it is made of the same substance in chemistry. Welcome change rather than fear it.

Since thinking is energy and perceptions are thinking than perceptions are energy. All is energy. Love is energy. Beliefs are energy. God is energy and in everything. life and death of everything is energy. The tree becomes many thing after its death as a tree and therefore continues to be energy. You too, take on new form and continue to be energy.

Marriage of Science and Religion

This is about the marriage of religion and science, something that both fields tried to avoid for years. Like church and state which cannot be separated either. Religion was always influencing politics and science was influencing religion. Go ahead and believe there is a separation or if you know there isn't that is ok too. Honoring where you are at is a must. You can't move ahead if you do not know where you are. It's ok where you are but know that there is excitement in discovering something new as it can be the high on life experience missing in your life.

You might want to read, "The Physics of Immortality" by Frank Tipler. It helped me understand more about energy and physics as a layman. This book cost him likely any promotion in his teaching career as the opposition was in science as was his colleagues. It did such a good job at joining the science and religion concepts. God gave me the book so to speak so that should count for something. Pioneers always have the opposition to deal with and it is never easy. This book is partly my autobiography as it tell somewhat of where I have journeyed in thinking and etc. You can relate to some of it but not all of it is likely. If no one agrees that is alright too as it is my beliefs and I am comfortable with that. A real friend said that everyone should write their autobiography as no one knows your life like you. You should like your journey and not wish you had done much of it different because everything leads to your next knowing of something.

The yet unknowns in science and religions made it possible for the two fields to look like they were separate for a time but now- with all the knowledge available to all there will be a marriage. There are also political reasons for each field not wanting to marriage and that is financial as science fights for grants from government and religion want tax exemption. That is no small feat. Neither science nor religion will be lost in the marriage as it is bound to happen. Tipler's book is one of the best corner stones that I found. There were a lot of unknowns to deal with like the soul, spirit and energy. Whose field did it belong in and they cannot be separated as they belong in both. We are primitive because neither field wanted to venture into these areas. soul, spirit and their connection to life was left in limbo making our progress in the meaning of life lagging. Meaning of life to become all you can become, was difficult.

Albert Einstein

To know that what is impenetrable to us really exists, manifesting itself as the highest wisdom and most radiant beauty which our dull faculties can comprehend only in their most primitive forms-this knowledge, this feeling is at the center of true religiousness. In this sense, and in this sense only, I belong to the devoutly religious men.S

This is the most beautiful quote for the marriage of science and religions that you can find. To move ahead, the two fields cannot be separate. You see soul, spirit and energy are all one as God and us are one. Try to see the air in the world as one and it can help you see that we are energy and all one. The Bible tries to tell us this but we see ourselves as separate and miss interpret or ignore or do not see it. As you gather more information about a subject you change your view of it. So stop just being a pew warmer in church and be challenging. In science know that you have just found the tip of the information. When Einstein solved the theory of relativity, I read that when his fellow scientist applied it to a new area, he fought them on it as he had not thought of it being used that way. Later he saw it to be ok. That is what we all should be open too, new information all the time on any subject. God is not dead but churches are. If churches want to be just a history lesson than encourage members to go out on their own to find God for themselves and not get stuck in history. Churches are very limited in finding a personal relationship with "God/It".

Soul, spirit and energy are easier to see as both science and religion today than in the past as we are more connected to each other and cell groups are forming all over the world. They call themselves spiritual rather than religious as I am one of them. Seeing them as both science and religion is not as difficult as both fields acknowledge the need to see the areas that cross over. It did not help that science saw themselves as the stronger field and religion was for the weak. My husband and children were both religious and in science as physics was their interest and did not seem to have a big issue with the marriage. We are all advancing our beliefs and none of them believe as I do. That is all right.

Example: I was recently informed of the Biblical encounters with prophecy that I had glossed over, having read the Bible cover to cover five times and missed. The encounter was about how many times the prophets used water or shinny objects to make decisions or see into the future. Now you might want to conclude that was primitive. Well study séances that were held in the White House especially with Lincoln and that he was told that he was in danger as was JFK. We also read that the priests of the temple used three-sided dice like objects to decide the answer to issues as they believed God was doing the deciding.

The Magi saw the star in the well(water) that they followed. You say but we are advanced and do not do that but are we advanced?? Nastrodamous used a bowl of water for his prophecies. It takes time to ponder these ideas rather than discount them. We have been taught to stay within the norm but norms change so be a changing agent. You are what you believe.

My daughter had de' ja vu since she was four years old, my son had dreams that came true until 18 when he had a dream that he did not want to come true so prayed all day to have it not so then asked God to take the dreams away and he stopped having them. I had the experience of leaving my body thru a vortex that I made each night at 7 and 8 years of age. These unaddressed spiritual experiences were not talked about in churches and therefore left in the air. My most vivid experience with others about the spirit world was when I was teaching six grade Sunday school and two students wanted to talk about their experience in having a séance in the church and a body was produced. I handled it poorly as it was a great opportunity to teach on spirit and I was not prepared. I did not tell them it did not happened and did not answer their questions well either.

I did go to my minister and he verified that it happened as the police were called. No body there when police got there! The children were open to answers but I did not have the answer and the minister, though knew of it happening did not expound on it either. SAD! Because it was not addressed in most churches it was thought to be evil. There is no devil for me, there is evil mostly in mankind. The spirit world will follow your beliefs or desires. What you fear you bring to you. I have felt evil three times and it was in mankind. My Pentecostal friends always talked to much about the devil or Satan and I struggled with that and prayed for the answers as I did not believe God needed an adversary, after all, God was the creator of all.

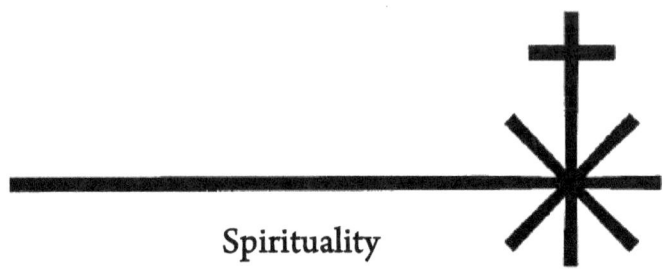

Spirituality

So why did the churches walk away from spirituality? Power and control were an issue and the unknowns were numerous just as they are today and were meant to be. Why? because we are all in different places in our walk of life and on different pages. Culturally we are not comfortable being out there on the limb by ourselves. Of course we are not as God is always with us. If you are like me, I sometimes tell God that I know "It" is always with me but I am a doubting Thomas so show me! God has a good sense of humor as I have tested him greatly. "It" is warm and fuzzy and if you do nothing else in this life time make.

Remember the witch hunts of Salem? The unknown has always been culturally a problem. The Pilgrims came to America for religious freedom and here is a blatant contradiction to what they were here for. Tolerance was not one of their strong points. Everyone had to follow the one belief or? Power and control was the desire and of course they were mostly women who were hunted down. Men wanted to power over. Since my Mother's family were Pilgrims and Quakers, I might have been one of the hunters or I could have been one of the hunters. This concept intrigues me. Why intrigues me? Because as human beings we are always in the process of becoming. If you have not experienced this you cannot know that. If you are ever asked if you can imagine yourself doing anything, the answer is always yes. If any human being is capable of doing something than you are. The likelihood of some of us doing a lot of things may be slim but as human beings we are all capable. Getting rid of ego teaches us that we are all capable of everything any other human being is.

Power and control usually is associated with wealth and that is an issue. Follow the money and find the insecurity. You think that wealth brings security but we only have to look at Hollywood to see how insecure most of them are. More is not better. The lottery is another example. If you earn what you have it has value and satisfaction. God, spirit, and etc. do not want or need money and you cannot take it with you. Having enough is a big lesson and not easy because we all want some excess to feel secure. To learn to have enough is to trust and have faith. We say we have trust and faith, but do we? It is really important to trust and have faith that everything is taken care of in the long run. I like it when a plan comes together. It is awesome and will increase your faith and trust that there is a God or higher power. My still small voice says, "Yes, it is awesome and you did not need it until zero hour ". You may want it before zero hour but that is not how faith and trust are built. Learning patience is a continuum in learning.

When I got in trouble in life, it was my thinking that was too serious, yes life is serious but should be more adventurous. See if that is happening to you. Step back and laugh at yourself for not having patience, trust, and faith in the universe really wanting to give you the desires of your heart. Not being Santa Claus but what you really need will come. What is really needed is the next key to your journey.

Trusting that it will all turn out the way it usually does and should. Faith that what you hoped for will come to the past. Patience that I did not need it until the need or zero hour. I now laugh and say that I am tired of hanging by my finger nails when it appears. We sure get the same experiences over and over some times and the reason is that to really incorporating something into our being and owning it is a process that needs practice, practice and more practice. That one issue in your life may be the main theme in your journey in this life to learn.

Example: I am in the same predicament today as was 36years ago. I needed to sell a home. Back then I threw a tantrum. It was a Sunday morning and I got up, did not go to church which was not like me. I vowed to sell the house that day for 10 cents if someone was willing to buy it. Now I was very vocal and it was to God. I sold that home that day for under market value. I had housing problems for the next 15 years so paid heavily for that tantrum. That home sold a couple years later for 10 times what I sold it for. Today I am at peace for the most part with the same need. I am out of my comfort zone but handling it with more patience, trust and faith, that all will happen in due time for me. Now I am fully responsible for all my decisions and God is not doing them, I am. So much of our situation we blame God and that is not "It" that is making the decisions. I believe our requests get honored if they line up with our life's process. No, might be the answer some like to say but I am glad when some requests do not get answered. I do not get everything I want, only what I need. Need can be much that I did not ask for but needed for my journey in growth and development. We need to reflect on our overall journey more to see life's purposes. It is an individual journey and being influenced by others is usually a mistake. The more advanced you are in a process the more you are asked to go it alone and that is not what flesh wants but is what spirit needs. Others do not have the answer for you only for themselves. It is good to have a different perspective but remember it is just that. Trusting oneself is the key and that is not always comfortable as we feel alone which we never are. God is always with us. Perfect timing is what happens when you are patient and in perfect timing you are the only one who knows what and when that is. It is awesome. If you are not in this spiritual understanding, you will feel alone in most of your decisions. It is not a comfortable place to be unless you know that you are never alone. The force is with you!! OR I like it when a plan comes together.

So looking at life as an adventure and being able to laugh at yourself will help you go on in your journey.

Having friends and family not agreeing with your decision makes it hard for us to believe we have made a sound decision but getting back to trust and faith in ourselves will come and we will be glad to have gone thru the process of uncertainty and moved on. It gets easier to go thru the uncertainty really. Not sure we ever get to like it as trust and faith does not come easy. This is the same as self-esteem and is important as a sense of high self-esteem will carry you a long way. Not something taught in our institutions for the most part and we miss out because of that. Families could do a better job also. Only you know what is in your best interest or where you are in your growth. You will get stronger as you really live your experiences with awareness. You do need to separate what flesh wants and what spirit is trying to help you remember in your script for coming to planet earth. God or spirit will not take you anywhere until you are ready and sometimes you may not know you are ready but it is the next need in your growth. Why are we all in different places on the path? Well our openness is the key. Open to new information and sometimes we are not. If you think you know the truth then for you do. That, however, may close the door to new knowledge. I like to think we know very little so to be open to expounding on what I know. I have said for some time that my life was a rehearsal, and it is and so is yours. Read Betty Eddie's book, "Embraced By the Light". A client of mine read it and was so relieved as it made sense and helped her look at her struggles and knew she would be ok. This was her script. You wonder why anyone would script what they experience but they do.

Our ways of learning are very diverse.

If we believed that most of our life is scripted, we would play with life more and not take ourselves so seriously. We would take the good with the bad. There is no good or bad as all our experiences teach us something therefore a benefit to our growth and development. If I learn something of value then how can it be bad? Culturally we are very negative. If you wonder why it is hard to be positive, look at what you take in in the day. Set out each day to turn the negatives into positives. It could be just smiling at someone who is sad or looking at your loss as another's gain. Just set out to smile all day and guess who will feel good at the end of the day. YOU! You get back what you give away.

The mind is everything. Every cell in your body has a mind of its own. The mind is not in the brain. The brain is the circuit of the mind or the pathways. Everything you need is within. You must change your thinking before you change your feelings or behavior. It is up to you.

We think permanence provides security which there is none as everything is in flux or impermanent. The meaning of life is to become all you can become. It doesn't say you have arrived you are in the making as everyone is. If we saw everyone on their journey, we would be less likely to think of right or wrong but just where they are at. No right or wrong. Love people where they are at not where you want them to be. Learn something new every day so you can see your growth. My brother told me yesterday, that the longer the electrical cord was the less circuit. I did not know that even thou it stands to reason. We will live life more fully if we look at everything as impermanence. It is the only thing we can count on. The universe tells us that change is the reality of all things. This is the key to being comfortable with death. The way to see death as positive is to look at Fall and Spring. Death and new birth.

The science way is that every subatomic interaction consists of the changing of the original particles and the creation of new subatomic particles. The subatomic world is a continual dance of creation and changes. The masses changing into energy and energy changing into mass. These changes create a never-ending new reality. I am not a scientist but this concept should be the bases of our belief of death.

Our lives are but this dance of transient forms. Everything is always changing forms as in the Spring and Fall as evident by the changes. A dance is a good thought for the death process. If we can have a good image, it will help and we should use it. Make it a fun image. "You are what you believe", so get rid of what is not working for you now. How do you know what isn't working for you now? If it leaves you troubled, sad, or worried etc. Find the, "piece that passes all understanding."

My definition of depression many times is the lack of action in our lives Both the physical and mental. Fear of change is high on the list for the lack of action. We are good at making excuses for not moving ahead with change. Worrying about this or that stop us from changing direction. Worry being one of the biggest waste of energy as three fourths of them never come to the past. Worry is negative so change it into challenges or your journey. Worry is the lack of adventure. Some people think worry is a sign.

It is deep love when it is a lack of trust and faith. If you are worried about your children, you have not transferred trust and faith in them to them. You are holding on to it as if it is up to you to save them. If you have taught them to be responsible for their decisions, they will do just fine. After the age of 13 we hopefully have given them the tools to make good decisions. Our children know by this time if we do trust them. So letting go and trusting is a parents lesson I contend that children teach us more than we teach them. Having children should be fun. Life is an adventure and hopefully we do not teach our children to do it our way or else as that is a fear tactic. Children need to trust that we are trustworthy. It is a sense of a "self" that makes a child do what is in there and communities' best interest with no resentment. Adults who have done it someone else's way do resent it in the end. That is why we come back to planet earth to do it differently. Ihe never ending story of eternal life. We change forms upon death but we still go on learning after death. Hitler as well as Jesus are both in heaven as that is all there is and they are still learning or helping the rest of us. Yes, spirit world does try to help us move to a better place in our evolving.

So venture into new beliefs and separate yourself from old beliefs. Be creative and have no fear of being wrong for we are always wrong, for there is always a different view around the corner. Once you realize you have what you need for today which is the goal for today and stay in the day you will find life more joy. It is when you think you have the answers that you stop your growth. This is to give you motivation and excitement in the next bend in the road of our adventure. If your adventure is squashed then you need to reclaim it. One way is to know that "It"/God has never left you but you may have dropped "It. It" has never left you as it is all around you and in you so it cannot leave you. You have heard of aura? If you have not then start by looking at it and do some studying of it on your own. I say on your own as it is important to gather some information on the subject then get others' opinion. Not the other way around.

I think of aura as a cloud, which is energy. (Thunder and lightning included). Now think of yourself encased in that cloud but this time it is warm and fuzzy. Now think of "It" around and in you. This energy. When you have a high on life experience this version is easy as that is what it feels like. You are encased in the warmth of "It" or the arms of "It" and you are. Our joy is God's joy at our discovery.

Please stop making God human as "It" is not. If you struggle with needing "It" to be personal, be creative but stay away from the human traits. You will likely grow by leaps.

The most fascinating aspect of everything is its energy. You do not have to be a physicist to look at the energy and mystery of everything. Not just electrical but physical energy. Take a look at your own energy both physical and mental. The physical is likely motivated by the mental, and the mental by your health. That is why getting enough sleep, eating well and attitude is primary.

Don't feel like doing something. Well change your mind and you can have the energy to do it and will be glad. The motivation maybe money but never the less it is mental. When you look at the aura which is energy in and around you which is connected to the whole of energy and everything than "It" is not so impersonal. There are as many ways of seeing it all as there are people.

We need to see how we have brought God down to our level which has hindered our growth and development. There was never a need to do that but power and control. The less in life that you need power or control over anything the freer you are in life. Free to be me comes when you no longer have to be controlling. This may be a troublesome phase as it may seem that you do not care about anything. Culturally we have loved drama so the new feeling of freedom takes some getting used to it too. For some the drama in life is what makes life exciting for some. But free of drama is more realistic and exciting. It is just a foreign feeling for a while. It is the difference between an air-filled balloon and a helium filled balloon. Free of drama is the helium balloon. You fly much higher and free. Helium is the spirit of all that is.

Helium is defined as "the sun" a chemical element, a colorless, odorless, very light, non-reactive gas having the lowest boiling point and melting point. Doesn't this just blow the mind? Isn't this a good reason for the marriage of science and religion? It works for me. Now to just elaborate on the description of helium as having the lowest boiling and melting point is this not a desire of the human being in situations and decision making?? It is hard to make a decision when having a meltdown.

When free of drama and emotions your decisions are purer. They are more objective but remember the observer affects the observation as no one is without an opinion. But it is likely that taking the "self" out of the equation as much as possible will help. Winning or being right is culturally killing us as we do not look beyond winning or losing or being right for being fair in all decisions. Greed and deception is killing America or has killed America as we see how sick our society is. The truth be known is that all this is more known than those in power and control understand. The violence in our streets today is not caused by guns. Guns do not act, it is the anger that tells us that the unfairness is coming to a head. The unfairness that we have embraced for years is payback time. What goes around does come around.

Greed comes about when one does not see that there is enough. How many millions do you need? Let me tell you, your health is far more important. Why do we publish who has the most money? We do it because that is what we chase to be identified as important. Will our crash make us become more equal? A path of destruction is hard to stop. It is like teaching our children not to lie as one lie leads to another to another.

It is then hard to remember how we got to where we are. I venture to guess that we in the US are lied to and told more propaganda than any other country. We have gotten so good at it that the truth is hard to find.

Example of craziness WAR! There are first no winners. The destruction is awful, the deaths and maimed outweigh any benefit, and pain and suffering are felt on both sides. Plus it is primitive and barbaric. The difficulty lies in how to stop a war. No war did it well. Bringing all the soldiers' home is a big issue as we see today. Money allocated for war is different than that for reintegrating Much less for reintegrating so where do these ex-fighting service people live, work, and get the help they need? This is a big problem when war has bankrupt the country already. Why not print more paper money and give each one a new start?

For me President Obama is a super hero but he inherited so many problems and has a congress that was all ego even he could not straighten out the mess. Hillary will have some of the same problems with the mess she inherits. Of course all the problems will be her fault and will be slanted for her being a women. This is 2015 and you can see how predictable and boring our news really is. You want youth to behave themselves when they see how adults behave and are selfish??

Get the old geezers out of the office and limit now the number of terms allowed. No career politicians any more who are bought and paid for by industries or interested parties.

One race for mayor in New York state elected a 25-year-old; a good sign of fed up with politics as usual and let's hope that this becomes a trend.

Conservative is a word used to attract the ignorant and that is on its way out also. Look it up in the dictionary and you will see it is about the good old days and there is none. Liberal means moving ahead and change. Liberal was used by politicians as a negative concept but look it up in the dictionary and it is progressive and a necessary ingredient in growth. Fear keeps things the same and falling apart. Republicans are giving Hillary the win do to their lack of organization and being blind to the needs of the country. Their behavior is really a disgrace to our nation. To take a giant step from ignorance all of this is necessary. Did we need a Hitler? Did we need two Bush's? Yes, we needed our eyes opened and we are all responsible for what has happened. Respect has left along with the common sense. I was a Republican for some 30 years but voted mostly independent because it was easy to see that money was driving the show with favors and kickback being common practice. Now! why are we in the toilet? We are very corrupt and have such a beautiful country. Personal gain is all ego and immature. We are adolescence at our best.

We have in our country really bright youth but they are baffled as to what and how they can fix it or make a difference as it is so fragmented.

Hillary will have a tough time knowing what can be fixed first. Youth see very clearly what is going on and we wonder why they are acting out. Ihe news makes it look like the blacks are the problem but they have less to lose and as you hear it is black phobia in the ingredients. White males do have of a fear of black power especially the ignorant (remember ignorant is lack of knowledge. Not stupid as we take it to mean.) Tie residue of poor knowledge and teachings from years past has kept black phobia alive for some white males in America. Blacks need to take some responsibility for their part too. Do not fight the establishment but get educated as many of you are and make a difference as our President has proved it can happen. We are not all blind to the need for change. Women and blacks are coming forward in politics and other fields. It was said that both had less brain power and were kept unsure of themselves. No one can do anything less we let them move ahead.

Our youth in the past had been our barometer for what needed to be change but the Kent State massacre took care of them and spoke out. This was our Teneman Square. If you look at our history, the 70's started our downhill decline. Ihe check and balance system was weakened. There really isn't any balance today so anything you can get away with is just a cleaver move.

Youth went into technology as a way to be something in society. as they now had more skills in it than the old geezers. But with the old still in power and control there was still no balance for everything went electronic and the danger in that has already proven to be disastrous. What happens when the computers go down? What happens when a bank closes its doors? What happens when information of all kinds is compromised? We still do not have a salutation as old methods are lost. What did we do before computers cannot be answered by most high school kids. They grew up with electronics. So my point is; how advanced are we? We will move to community by forces to be, namely a financial crash. We will have to help each other through it. Adolescence is our selfish period and community is when we become aware that the others are needed to complete the whole picture. We are all one.

Hillary will inherit a mess but with the feminine side which is much more "Godly", women will embarrass men into being fairer. Churches are made up of older women led mostly by men.

Women are coming into their own but not to dominate but to equalize. Just saw a documentary on the WWII "WAVES" They were women who were pilots in the war. They were real good pilots but never part of the recognized military. Sixty-seven years later Obama signed a bill giving them recognition The same happened to women in the factories. They were a part of a male dominate society. Some of these women are still alive and, in their 90,'s. We will not do this to males this time in history as we do not need to be that controlling. Churches will just have to adjust and many will fight it by Bible thumping but we have had enough of that. God never intended dominance over or "IT" would have that behavior and does not. Unconditional love does not dominate or need too. We have blamed God for years but it is the evil in man and there is enough in the human. No, the devil did not make you do it. There is no devil, just evil in mankind. Power and control told history the way they wanted to The story of the Indian and Blacks have been distorted also. Who were the savages?

Women have their work cut out for them as they train men to be less in need to control, be right in everything, have power over, have the answer for everyone, angry and bossy. Women are responsible for letting it go on for so long but for many they still like to be taken care of. Transitions are difficult and slow to take hold. It was women who went to church and supported the church which was for years a male dominated institution. Go into church today and the women outnumber the men and it the older women. and youth just do not fit in with its out of date messages. Maybe the church as a foundation is all it can be. The puzzling part for me is the lack of real influence in real life for we still have wars, more corruption, and less happiness it seems. I had to find the church within or stop growing so left the church not that long ago. God does not dwell in churches but in the heart if everything, humans, animals, plants, and etc. For "It" is energy In the Bible it tells that David was not to build a temple as God did not reside in buildings so look at the heart of a person to know where their Godliness is. To say one thing and do another is what is happening too much of the time. God will not judge you but you will upon death.

This leads to the fact that we believe what we are told and investigate very little as to why we want to believe something. There is no excuse for not looking up a belief, you have to see its history and if it is for today. Reading is a must. Men are less likely to read than women. Publishing firms promote male authors more than not but self-publishing has helped in publishing today. See control even in this and do you know who own the big publishing firms? Look it up. Who owns movie companies? The money trail is influencing and controlling old or popular trends. Men are more likely to be couch potatoes and watching this promotion of the same old ideas of men being superior. In transition there will be more anger at women by men as they change their old thinking.

I have a 98year old male friend who reads newspapers each day and has a sharp mind. Reading you might say is his best friend and he loves to talk if he can find someone to listen to. Do we like to listen? What I observe in him that is different from most men is that he has something to say that he see as value. Most men do not feel they have anything to say of value. Now that is learned in life as everyone has a history and story to tell. My 98-year-old friend has a fascinating history and I and my daughter wanted to write his story as he was like a Tom Sawyer.

When we read, we need to keep in mind that is someone else's version of the read. It should add a dimension to your life. What you focus on you bring to you. The reading that brings meaning are not love stories that makes you feel like you are lacking something in your life but history, true life stories and the Bible as a history book. The bible is a good history book and is fascinating for me as a human behaviorist, as if read cover to cover you see how we have evolved in our thinking. It is a good reference book for seeing the beliefs of the time and how we have changed. I have wondered how many bible thumper have read it cover to cover to discover the evolving of history. My reading it cover to cover five times was a real blessing in history and changing times. God became a present moment experience for me. Remember Jesus came to help change the times as things were going in the wrong direction. Do you know what and who it was that was not teaching the truth of God?

God always sends someone or something to correct us on our path today as "It" did in days of old. Writing this book makes me feel close to God and all the experiences, which are many in my journey so far. History is just that a view of what helped us move ahead to different beliefs and ideas. Look at our civil war or any of our personal wars or our financial crisis present and come to see how thinking changes. How do I know we are heading for financial crisis? The Bible tells me so. It says that you cannot keep going down the wrong path before it catches up with you. Common sense.

After every war personal or foreign, there are big adjustments and they are never easy to go through. How long ago was the civil war? We are still adjusting to it. Our belief systems get challenged Some can adjust and other cannot. There is a need to make room for new ideas, behaviors and feelings. If war has any value, it is this change that it produces. It is said the only secure idea is that change is inevitable. So let's welcome it and stop fearing it.

So the only guarantee in life is change. Our culture is dominated by those who fear change as they see it as a loss rather than a gain. Politicians use the word conservative to gain votes or popularity from those who do not want to change or move forward. Not moving forward usually just delays the inevitable and it is usually costly in many ways such as emotional, behavioral and financial. Selfish gains are usually at the route of not moving forward. This might be a good time to examine your life to see if you fight moving forward and why? Has being conservative kept you in your comfort zone and stopped progress? You may say you do not have time to ponder. Well I have had many revelation while driving on long solitary trips. I used to say when I turned the key on," Well God what are we going to look at on this trip?" I did not like the radio on, just listened to that still small voice.

Well I was coming back from my mother's (she died in 2000) when I heard the still small voice say," If Jesus comes again what will it be called?" Now I knew that voice and just what it was wanting me to say. I am a little bit of a brat, so said the standard reply, "that it was Jesus' second coming. "In the same tone the voice repeated "If Jesus come again what will it be called." With this I replied, "the reincarnated Jesus" There was silence and I started to cry. Remember I knew what God wanted me to deal with as a few years before I was confronted with reincarnation and asked if we could table it for a while. The desire was granted but now it was time. Mind you I believe I always believed in more than one life. I stopped crying and said I was ready to deal with reincarnation now. I then went to study everything I could on reincarnation. A wonderful journey into history, the church squashing it and the bible was very helpful. Like magic I am led to what I need to grow and learn. Matthew 1-13 is called the transfiguration but it is a spiritual picture of the disciples and their natural belief in the return of those who die and reincarnation. Who would they have built a tent for? Spirits? They saw Moses and Elijah in the flesh. Materialized as real. Remember Jesus does it after his death too. Reincarnation was a natural belief of the time as many believe today. God gives as many revelations as possible today and maybe more than "It" did in years of old. Some churches have as part of their service a telling of what God has done in your life like an answer to prayer and etc. It helps to be part of a group that is seeking God's direction and does not have God only of old. A present-day God.

Now you likely already get revelations but may not call them that, you may say you had a light bulb moment or answer to prayer. Since God never leaves you or forsakes you, there is an influence there for your knowledge to increase. Tie words we use or do not use are of great influence and we use so many words to mean what is not a good picture of what we want or need. Take the word reincarnation or evolution. Due to Darwin's theory which at the time the churches felt threatened by it so it got a negative tone. We are evolving like it or not. You were born a baby, became a toddler, young adult etc. Use the word change and evolve interchanging to get used to it and take it back as a positive word. See how powerful words can be if used to mean negative or positive. God taught me that words are very powerful and let me tell you I struggled with that. I need is different than I want. I learned that just to change the words, "I want to I choose to". I liked to say, "that you know what I mean" before learning the power of correct words. The dictionary is never far from me as now I am in the habit of looking up the meaning of words. is how I got "It" as God, the impersonal force. Maybe if you really realized that God/ "It" is in everything you do, you would see that you are in continuous prayer as you reflex on what is the Godly thing to do in each thing you do. When I was young, I used formal prayers but as I got older my prayers were just talking to God as I do you. I try not to beg God for something which is hard as I feel it urgent but God does not. God for me is warm and fuzzy. Also has a big sense of humor. I say "It" needs it to deal with my questions. Did you ever read to your children, "It's Me Margaret?" Well I say, "get your humor cap on God it is me, Lois. It" does. This makes God and my relationship very light hearted and personal and increased the energy around me. I feel encased in the energy of God. If you say that there is a serious side of life, well I can only half agree as we are meant to take the good with the bad and see it all necessary. See the bad as a good teaching tool. Bad things happen for a good reason. Bad things happen to good people. Why? Because we need the experience. In adversity we learn the most.

I have lived in a place for 28 years that I have not liked but I have learned the most from being set aside to have time to read, study and therefore it was all good. I understand it all. I choose to grow and remember so here I am in the right place. It is all in the perspective. Isolation can teach you more because you have the time to go within. Everything you need is within.

I had a job that I really enjoyed, which was as a psychotherapist. I did not like psychiatry as I felt it did more harm than good in helping people with depression or anxiety to move forward. Medicine was the treatment of choice and it was relied on too much. It took away the symptoms but does not treat the problem. Too much reliance on meds became the choice. This led me to stand on my own convictions and study human behavior in many ways that psychiatrists may not have time too or do not want too.

Our careers or fields we go in do give us a mindset that can be confiding. I take a holistic approach to it all as my education fostered that kind of thinking. Body, mind and soul approach.

To grow it does take time alone and we all need to take that time back. I just heard that in a survey the college student said that the most important thing in their life was not money but to be happy. We are getting to a bend in the road that is long overdue. I am big on learning and studying forever as that is what you can take with you when you leave this earth and form.

It may be a good sense of self that is needed to feel good about being alone with oneself. In my family we talk about loving people but liking to be alone too. My parents seemed very comfortable and independent and did not see outsiders for days. They were farmers and of course that was demanding work But they seemed to be alright with whatever came down the pike. So you are a product of your environment. Our job in adulthood is to look at what we experienced and add to it, expound upon it or throw out what does not work for us now. We would grow much faster if we just believed that sooner not later in life. It should be taught in our rights of passage years.

So welcome change and have fun with it. Change the thinking therefore the feelings and then the behavior will change. Magic!! The mind is a powerful tool and it all begins with thinking. Feelings are produced by thoughts and are said to be the language of the soul. Words are formulated to produce or express feelings and then behaviors are our actions on those thoughts. If feelings are the language of the soul then we should not run away from any feelings those we claim that are bad or good. In panic attacks this is very important. These very strong feelings deal with our fears. Our need to deal with our fear> is a major part of our life's growth. You have total control over your fears. Yes, you do! It may not think you do but that is it changes your thinking about the fear. If the language of the soul; what does your soul want and you need? I would guess that it want you to take back your freedom of that fear. Now most of my panic disorder clients were Catholics. Why? discovered this not me. Clues; soul, truth, freedom and not really knowing God. The greatest fear is around death and dying. Most fear how they will die rather than death. If you believe in hell and the devil you will likely fear death and judgment.

Hell there is none. Shakespeare said there is no hell lest you make there one. Remember you are what you believe. The reason for panic attacks. So why keep the control in your beliefs system that give you such a reaction in the body. Most of history is just that history for the learning of the times That is why most growth requires some knowledge of history. Did you realize that the Catholic church told its parishioners that they needed to leave the bible up to the priest to interrupt that was when I grew up and maybe still do. Know why?

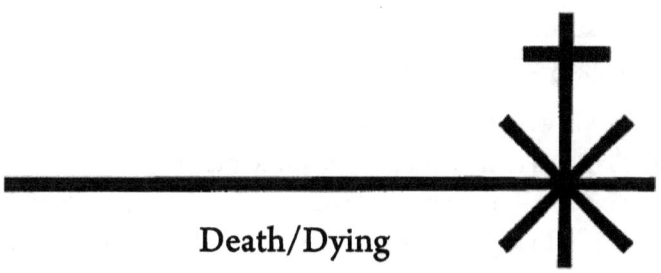

Death/Dying

So if birth is positive than so is death. Let's find a way of thinking positive. How about starting with there is no death. You have eternal life. What does eternal life mean since churches do not do a good job at preaching this but say they believe it. More time needs to be spent on these important topics. Since each will interrupt it their way that alone takes control out of the picture for others to control you. Now you have a chance to change your thinking. What and who controls your thinking? Lest you make their one really means that it is up to you what you believe. Is that scary? Since most of us do not think for themselves.

Remember you can know something but not be able to live it. Head knowledge comes before heart knowledge and by heart knowledge, I mean be able to live the knowledge. My sense of humor just said that some of this knowing for Lois is still more knowledge than I am able to act on at least all the time. My flesh is still active. Soul and flesh might help you see eternal life more fully if you see yourself just changing forms at death. that is, you become soul/spirit. So when you die you will experience your beliefs so anything that gives you anxiety changes before you die. Life is serious and hard work if you do not want to take the time to explore new ideas for your beliefs and death. Many people have long sicknesses before death. Why?

It might be that they are waiting for family and friends to get ready to release them but it might be that they are coming to terms with their death and dying issues. It is said by whom I do not know that we give permission to die. Why would someone want to be murdered, tortured, have a long sickness, a car crash or any number of ways to die. We all would like a quick no pain death. That is an issue but the way around it is to change your beliefs about death and its purpose.

Why do you want there to be a hell? Maybe you want all the bad guys to get theirs. Well remember Do unto others as you want unto you. Maybe they want there to be hell so you get your just reward. It is all in the perspective. Pray for your enemies and wish them well. A lot of work there.

Let's talk about judgment day, there again it is not what I was taught. First, I want to say that upon death there are no emotions. Those are human traits. Spirit does not have them but does understand them. So the judging is done by you and all the beliefs that life was about success, money, fame, even how good you were to others and all your sacrifices will be purified by you. Let's say you did all those good things for others at your experience as if you had too. Not pure! You will see why you did what you did. Because someone else said so will not fly. Now I am sure you do not like me at all. Lying is what we do a lot to ourselves to excuse our beliefs. Now I am a doubting Thomas so the search for the answers for me was long and extensive and unless the peace that passes all understanding came I kept on searching as I knew there was a piece missing yet. The piece missing was always key to the concept. Awesome! The peace that passes all understanding is like the high on life experience or a light bulb experience. Buddha under the tree experienced it when his revelation moment came. It's a way of life after that or the path now followed.

An example of thinking that is harmful is victimization in any experience. It is a process to get over it but to remain angry and hold on to it for life is harmful to you. You need to change your thinking and to do that you must move from victimization to being the survivor. I did not say it is easy to get rid of the feelings that you deserved it or you were being punished for something is a thinking pattern that may be hard to break.

Why do you want to hold on to the victimization, what secondary gains are there from it that you like. Maybe it's the poor me, or other attention like how unworthy you are varied. If we do not see ourselves as worthy of better treatment than moving beyond it will be hard Forgive your enemies and pray for them. One sure way of getting over something is praying for what you see as your enemies. Bad things happen for a good reason and the reason may be just the process of getting over it. It can be a lifetime in the learning. A question I was asked a lot was, "I already experienced that why again?" Well the universe want to make sure you learned it and it is now part of your Being. Sit for a minute and ask yourself what do I in my life keep experiencing? It is likely a big part of your remembering this time around. I have a couple I do not like!!

Again what are the habits or benefits in victimization. Secondary gains we sometimes call them. You may think it is cruel to say anyone would have secondary gains in being a victim but when we hold onto something over a period of time or want to share it all the time, we want to then dissect it and ask ourselves why we still won't let go. Have you ever been for the underdog? Played devil's advocate?

Looking from a different point of view helps see the perspective from the other point of view. Why did that person feel a need to victimize you. It many times has nothing to do with you. You were just there at the time of their need. So try to see that it is not about your helps. We are the most violent society in the world. WOW! What is behind it? Anger, seeing things unfair, hurt, pain, immaturity, and usually some form of being a victim themselves.

A person I know was a victim by a care giver and loves to play poor me, that person is now a felon, in jail, and angry. That person when a kid lied in court to stay with the abuser. A phenomena that happens all the time and court or law guardians do not seem to catch. It takes a village to raise a child and in this case lots of mistakes were made and many tried to help. So as I see it this now adult person needs to stop thinking that what it's doing is getting even with the abuser and see that the one getting hurt is self and society. You have to believe that their journey in all of this is about their learning and maybe society will too. Drug addicts, rapist, and etc. are angry people. Why are they angry? They are abusive as they were abused. A cycle that does not seem to get enough attention.

There is no hell, lest you make there one and many do just that. Now there is really no hell as why a creator of everything would need a hell. Man made this up. The creator is Omni, meaning the all and everything. In everything and why would God put self in hell? Or need a hell? God created man and why did "It" do such a poor job? "It" did not, it is wonderful to see man grow and develop. I loved psychotherapy for this reason. Here is a chance for changing your thinking. You are perfect in "Its" image. You are right where you are supposed to be for now. Ask yourself if you are where you want to be as only you can change it and God really does not care. God is unconditional love.

Peeling away the layers to find that perfect self is what life has to give. Tie real self, the perfect self and the authentic self. You can choose to make yourself a new every day.

The devil was another crazy idea made up by man as God does not need a foe and neither do you. We are innately possible of doing all things. Neat! But not in one lifetime! God does not need an adversary and neither do you. There is not a battle going on as there is no need to be. You may wrestle with self and likely do in most of your major decisions in life. Think why you would need a devil or anyone else but you. We all make decisions from experiences, fear, logic, or because of our research. Thinking is still the powerhouse and it can seem to be one way and yet another. We have all thought that someone was mad at us and they were not. If it is positive, you are more likely on the right track. The soul wants to help you move ahead and into more reality. It will delight the soul, God/ "It" and the heavenly bodies to see you do the processing of thoughts and ideas. Don't settle for stale ideas for the highs on life are those that do just that, take us to a higher or different way of thinking. For too long we have paid little attention to why and what we believe and do. We have relied on others who are so-called authorities when they themselves are stuck. Comfort zones for everyone are different and a reason for not changing is likely the cost; cost economically, emotionally or fearing change. So that is why bad thing sometimes happen to good people. They need to shake us up and help us move on. If you were into what and why more it is not difficult to see that others are too and our results are all a product of our knowledge, beliefs and experiences. Therefore one may not be any better than the next. A good reason to trust your own judgment is because your journey is unique. We do not see our uniqueness due to looking outside ourselves.

We need more everyday folks active in what is happening as it always the few who run the institutions and the rest except what is concluded. We need more discussion groups that are willing to think out of the box and are not conservative. Conservative - no growth, why did the world ever get so much power? The answer is in a reason why we are stuck. If I keep you thinking that you live in the greatest country in the world and you better think that way or you are unpatriotic. and what you have is good enough and you are lucky to have it than you do not strive for different until you are angry, depressed or willing to take measures into your own hand. Taking measures into their own hands is what youth are trying to do in violence in the street and the drug scene starts out to be a way of making money, that which is worshiped and then becomes the controller. They are smart kids just fed up with adults that are not doing anything about the greed, corruption, dishonesty, back biting and selfishness. So join them if you can't fight any other way. You tell me the difference between greed and corruption at the top and in the streets. These kids have seen it and are taking the only way out they can see. They hate unfairness. Let's turn that around to being as adults, unselfish, fair, just, honest and kind to others. We are the laughing stock in the world right now as our campaigning for president of US just reached its lowest. (2016). What happens to one of us happens to all. Greed and corruption cannot be seen as success. Money has no value right now- really and figuratively.

Live by the sword -die by the sword so watch out what you worship.

We really do need the community concept and let go of adolescence. It is catching on but slowly. College students as I said just said," that being happy was more important than money". Did you just hear Wall street cry? I did as the more you give to pensions and most institutions the more they have to fuel their drive. It may not be your drive or even what you morally would want back. The rich are getting richer and more selfish. Now I have no problem with getting rich but I have problems with what you might be

doing or not doing it. I like philanthropy. and the love of mankind. Philanthropists are the only people that should get rich!!!

Did I tell you my sense of humor was unique?

If we are adolescents then it stands to reason that the youth do not have much to emulate. Present day adults have the problem not the youth. Look at what you looked up to when you grew up? Patriotism was big when I grew up not the flag, military or authority but the heart felt belief that people were good and would act accordingly. My parents were good, poor, hardworking, fair people and my trust in them was solid. Trust cannot be there today with all the greed. So where to begin right in your own heart. Take back your power and control by cleaning up within. Your belief system. GO COLLEGE STUDENTS you are on the right track. Propaganda, which is described as the wide spread promoting of an idea has been the root of our greed and corruption. Males in our culture are insulated in lies. Why? First, it was widely acceptable in the male world. Next, it is hard for males to confront males. And more than likely their beliefs were that if they got away with it, it was just a cleaver move. The lack of confronting has long been a silent code in the male world. Can you see the imbalance of power without women's influence. This code has hurt them in their growth and development. The young males are the ones that are now paying for this code as they see it and do not know in what direction to go. They know it is not money but money is still dictating. Young males seem to be unmotivated. Sports seem to be the only outlet and if you don't fit in there what is left for you as males? So anger and violence seem to be a way of fighting back.

Females are now moving into the once dominated male fields and coming into their own. Most vets are now females and when I grew up on the farm it was never thought of. Change is the only thing certain in our lives. The reason for the successful recruiting by the Taliban of youth is no different than the unhappiness in our culture. Angry at the status quo is the same in all youth. So treating the symptoms without looking at the cause is not working. Change does not happen at the top as they will just try to reinvent the wheel again and do not know any better. New ideas and blood are needed as we think out of the box, not conservative.

Stop using that word as there are no good old days. Youth will think out of the box and be more creative to move us forward. Have more youth discussion groups when we are in trouble as we are today. Most old geezers do not know that listening to the youth of our culture is the answer. Remember Kent State and the period when we squashed them. I have to remind you of the story of a tractor trailer that got stuck in NY city under an under pass and several males stood around and did not know what to do. A young boy came alone and just said let the air out of the tires.

WASP are really lagging and they know it so they just fight back like the youth do. WASP in America are the minority on the front lines and are conservative but I do not see them with the real conservative morals. A big symptom in our culture. Look at the exposure today of greed and corruption in the news. As time goes on and the balance of power is more in place we will see more of it as it will get worse before it gets better. What we get away with is just a cleaver move. With a balance of power there will be less corruption. What good are millions in death? You cannot take it with you when you go so have the delight of sharing it while you can. I can tell you when you are watching what happens after your, death with your money or what you worshiped in life will be an eye opener. Mediate on that. Greed is an illness that affects us all. We are one. Give me flowers when I am alive because I won't care when I die. I love flowers in a garden for all to see and enjoy so plant a flower for me when I die and I will come visit it in spirit.

Until we see that we are all one and what affects one affects all there is and will be separations from what we do and think. Love is all there is and let's start by forgiving ourselves for not loving everyone as self and really love unselfishly. God is unconditional love in everything and everyone. "It" may not like what you do but loves you unconditionally. You do not sin against God as you can't for God needs nothing from you. Why would "It"? "It" has everything and created it all in all its cycles. The cycles are the natural laws. What goes around comes around is a natural cycle. God put it in motion and it is law now. Spring will follow the winter. "IT" did not make a mistake even in making you. Love yourself for that reason. The natural laws are brilliant and fair to everyone and nature.

God is Unconditional Love

Let's dissect love mainly unconditional love, the love of God for it's creation all of it. There are no favorites. There is no right or wrong; good or bad; as that would be having favorites. No people or religions are favorites. This is hard for many to believe but must to move on and forgive. There are as many ways as there are people. So it is personal to believe. It may not be what you were told growing up but that was to help you get started in life and as we get older we have to decide for ourselves what works for us. If it does not work for you now think out of the box and create anew. We have been so used to letting others think for us and all those special interest laws are not helping as we find our way with change as thinking for oneself is taken out of play. We are all in the same playing field whether black, white, rich, poor, Muslim, Christian, artist, or scientist, as there is no better or worse. It is all part of the whole with all sorts of opportunities for growth and development. We as in nature have all sorts of different abilities and talents. Our talents have been called gifts as they are. No favorites in this as we all have different talents for our journey as teaching tools. It is ok to wish you could do something someone else does well but it may not be your talent If we honor our own we will honor everyone else. So we need to start with self, our own respect for self, as love and respect for oneself is needed to begin. Love, trust, and respect is needed more in our world, not just for those that believe as we do but with all human being as we are all one and all God's children. God does not have favorites so no class or race has it any better than another and that is hard to understand in a culture that has such a long wish list for not liking ourselves. We all live at this time and die to take with us what we learned this time around from what we were given not a wish list. We take nothing with us except what we did to advance our Being and the service to others along the way.

We need science to help us know the natural laws and spirituality to understand purpose and meaning in life. I did not say religion as it in it's present form it is just a foundation and a history in thinking which for many can be a stumbling block. At a certain point we graduate from church as we find our own beliefs but it is alright to use it socially as a group of people that we can relate too until we can't.

If churches are to survive they need to be more current and use history as a teaching tool rather than keeping people stuck and afraid to move ahead or into present day. God did not die two thousand plus years ago, as history is not a place to get stuck. My studying human behavior and it's history was fascinating but for me useless for the most part in my doing psychotherapy. I had to do it for the present times. We did psycho- analysis for years and clients stayed stuck in toilet training for years without moving on and then we went to blaming parents for years and they got stuck there so today we use the NOW therapies and they really work better. I liked cognitive behavioral therapy for me it worked. But it may be outdated some day. So we are evolving with the help of history. Creativity is getting lost in our culture and that scares me. We need to think out of the box and this is not encouraged by religions and science has it struggles with also. I like the "Big Bang Theory" as it is about that struggle. The history of science started in religion as religion controlled the universities and money. The study of Christianity and science were one and the same in the early years of their history. Look at Socrates, Galileo, and the struggle with the mindset of that day. How about a flat earth? Every field has a history that is hard for us to believe but that was the belief of that day and in the future others will find our beliefs of today archaic too. As we uncover more facts about our world we have to change our beliefs. Our existence is fruitless without new discoveries. Those who want to keep things as they are or were are failing to see that discoveries bring about new ideologies We add new dominions to the old. If we did not see right or wrong we would not be thinking that we missed the mark in the old thinking just needed more facts. Personal discoveries are just as important and happen the same way and for the same reason; to move our thinking along. That is why it is very important to look at our views of God. Humans are always changing but God does not but our views of God do change. New discoveries are inevitable so do yourself a favor and start being comfortable with change.

I sat in church for 15 years after I knew that my spiritual life was going no where. I was usually very active in churches I attended but if you are not growing spiritually it is all for not and you feel it as I changed churches three times in 15 years. Certainly said I was looking for growth. God was always at the center of my life but it was stale.

Good Friday was always a tough time for me and the last Good Friday in church I struggled with the same old same old. I went home and wrote the sermon over to my understanding. It was a light bulb experience that really helped me take a deeper journey into spiritually. I had already been to most churches and each had failed to satisfy my quest for a deeper meaning for life. Difference in churches are not significant as rules, dogma, and view of God as a punitive God, just is not unconditional love. Now at this time in my life I am reading 50 books a year and mostly on human behavior, spirituality, and science. I had for 40 years been a self healer. Books were the only way to find the others. Those who believed as I did or was believing.

Had you ever thought what if I did not make this or that decision where would I be? Well, today I know that I could not have missed what I was here to learn and grow with. Circumstances for my journey were in my face so much of the time that when I was ready I moved on. Did you ever wonder why the same people, situations and etc. are in your face all the time? Well they are clues about your need to change your views of them.

Doing psychotherapy for years, clients would come in with the same problems as before just a different twist to it. Why? Well the universe wanted them to be sure they had understood the problem or lesson to learn. We are either being tested again or we have not gotten it down pat yet. Do not fret it gets easier each time. Love is all there is so it will likely entail being more loving or positive. Reality is changing all the time but arriving at a more positive reality is likely going to get you the piece that passes all understanding.

If you have read the Bible cover to cover you will see that none of this contradicts the Christian beliefs. Interpretation is just that and you can only come from what you believe and so it is with everyone else.

If you are reading it is someone else's interpretation of what ever. So what you need to do is dissect it and see if it fits your belief system. A new thought may come to add to your already ideas. Everyone is not nor should they, think alike. We are all here on planet earth to learn different concepts and ideas; no wrong or right as for to long our teachings have sounded as if there was a right way that fits all. It is control and power that wants us to think alike. You are only accountable for your own journey. You will not be asked to account for anyone else but your treatment of other does count. I cannot wait to see how I affected others as you can never really know. If you meant good in your presentation and someone took it wrong or not as intended than they are responsible not you. That is why clarification is so important in communication.

A sense of humor is important on someone else's bad hair days where some take every thing wrong or wants to just challenge everything you say. It is exhausting but keep laughing internally will help. It is not you with the problem. If someone tells you that you made them mad. Do not defend yourself just ask them to repeat what it was that made them mad. Usually as they repeat it they can see their interpretation is maybe not as you intended. Intentions are everything so stop defending yourself if you are misunderstood. We should feel comfortable in asking for clarification. If you were having a bad hair day and moody, just fess up and say sorry no need to go into details as it take away from you. I notice when I am tired everything is more likely to go wrong as I have negative energy.

Our job in life is to know self, how else will we know God or others. I know when I am unconditional love and therefore know God. It is an awesome feeling; a feeling of the soul. So it is a soul moment. This does not need to be a fleeing moment as you can learn to both in for sometime.

I remember while counseling others, I would know when ego was gone and I was being pure me, the real me not ego. It was awesome and a soul moment too. I am a hypnotist and it is like being hypnotized or having an out of body experience. Getting self out of the way is or can be learned. Maybe you can recall having these moments. Relive them will help as you are recognizing the experiences and you are believing.

The more you practice the more you are affrming your beliefs and the more they increase. It can be fun to be aware as they happen. The mystery is that you however do not make them happen, it is your progression in beliefs that now you are in the knowing. God does know before you likely do that you are in the knowing or ready for the knowing. God never forces our beliefs, we are either ready for new concept or we are not. When you ponder that is good as it is part of the process. So it is in knowing or really really believing that is the key to the change. Prayers are answered at all levels of beliefs as God meets you where you are at. So because I believe that the rock is going to bring me water and truly believe than it will. This is the mystery of faith and life. We act out what we believe. Can't say this enough. You are what you believe. Stay where you are until you do not want to be there. No right or wrong, just are. AWESOME!

So all we need is in all of us, it is within as the Bible talks about all the time. You wrestle with self when you are in a quandary as the power and decision is in your beliefs and your thinking. Remember that the definition of insanity is doing the same thing over and over the same way wishing different results. If you are doing that than your thinking has to change for different results. If you are depressed, bored or whatever it will require a change of thinking than behavior will change and you are on your way to a different results, hopefully one that gives you a lift, joy or high on life experience. People who feel trapped in circumstances need to make a change or shift in thinking which will bring about an out and not be trapped. That is why it is said to break loose, is to give away what you want. If sad today go out and make someone's day by maybe just a smile or recognizing or acknowledging them. What you give away comes back to you in joy.

Now if you want to be miserable or poor me than recognizing that is what you want to get attention, so be it. No right or wrong. If a client came into therapy and the story was the same over a good length of time I would tell them that we have addressed this for sometime and they were not ready to change it so let's table it until they were ready. Tie first step, in taking responsibility for their feelings. I or anyone else was not responsible for their change they were. So again it points to in us.

As new information is added to our beliefs we need to be flexible as discoveries are always in the works and why wouldn't they be? We need to believe that a journey has surprises around each bend and is not static. If you think you know and have the answers already than you stop any information from coming forth except by force. Like when bad thing happen to good people. It usually changes a lot of beliefs. That was one for me as I was such a people pleaser. I needed to look at a lot of my behavior in a different way. It did not fit me any more. Not right or wrong just not working for me now. The norm of today was never meant to be the norm forever. Time changes all. Of course there is no time, just Now. The best attitude we can have is that things are always changing and enjoy the ides. What was for yesterday was for yesterday and tomorrow is a new day. If you think you have the answer than you will not question, why do I belief this or that. We have an innate desire to be like everyone else so if it is popular belief than we join the chorus There is power and control if you do not question for others in your life.

"It" Is God

So what does this have to do with God being "It"? We are co creator with God and you were created for a purpose and to see yourself as being created and there being a creator that helps you see the mysteries of life, let's you know that you are not alone in your journey. If we are believing we are co creators than it helps us move along with what we were given at birth. If we know where our talents lie we can develop them and use them more fully with joy knowing that they are gifts in our life.

It is not stressed or developed enough at an early age at being creative. Those who are encouraged to be creative are at an advantage. Electronics maybe seen as creative but are they? They encourage sameness as the programming is in there to find and everyone ends up in sameness. Schools should be more helpful and teach different ness as good and now with common core it is going in the wrong direction. We just like everyone predictable and alike. The masses are easier to control. Common core seems to be someone's ego child. It stops creativity rather than foster creativity. Many bright students at a,young age are bored in school so do not pay attention and get labeled incorrectly. I have two very bright sons and when in grade school the teacher and I decided to have her, the teacher just slip them more work when they finished before others and got restless. I'll bet it would be hard to get that happening today. It worked like a charm. The teacher and I were creative. No Ridlan needed. Be eager for the new and change. It is the difference between the living and the walking dead. Life really begins when you pay attention to it. Otherwise you are just going through the motions of life like sleep walking. The living see life with purpose and meaning and are usually upbeat and more positive about life. The walking dead see things very negative and have no clue as to why they are on planet earth. To live is joy. Taking life less serious is joy. Laughing a lot at nothing is joy. Why wait for something to laugh at; find laughter with flowers, trees, animals and people who are different as they are in your life for joy. Life is what we make of it and everything is a choice. You choose happiness as well as drama, sadness and etc... If you have a hard time believing this just think of others who go through what you do and how they handle it differently. The differentness is a choice. A learned choice through experiences or importance. Do not sweat the small stuff as it is all small stuff, maybe helps with placing things in importance. Wishing something didn't happen after it has is foolish but we do it a lot. Now accepting it is first step in dealing with it. We need to be fascinated with how others think not wanting them to think as we do. It would leave no room for growth if we were all alike. That is why those people that irritate you are in your face. A good reason to help you hone your being and the beauty of differentness. Accepting is not settling for something but gives you a chance to look at your own beliefs. You might not do that if those irritating people are not around. So thank them for being in your face. It is not easy to get there but if you first accept that you do not like that feeling than it is easier to go beyond it. I sometimes feel that I should not have the feeling that I do in the first place but then realize that being human is what I am and will have the feelings I do so acknowledging the feelings is the first step to change.

How you identify yourself is key to your life. I am a rescuer and a giver and it is not something that you can just decide not to do. You must learn how it works. My biggest lesson was to see when helping was hurting.

There are times when we need to let others find their way without help from us as they will not learn to move ahead in their thinking and life's journey. It is something that you have to stay on top of all the time. Tough love is just that, letting go of the need to rescue. Men in our culture want to solve the problems and move on when they need to teach and be patient It is hard to see others in need and not help. I have learned to be there for them once or twice but then know that they need to find the solution for themselves. If you understand your journey more you will understand theirs more. In therapy the therapist are not making decisions for clients but giving them options or food for thought that is good direction enabling them to find their own way. If someone is telling you the same story over and over then it is time to tell them that they are not ready to make a decision on it and to table it for now. Now big changes like a death, divorce and a real disaster takes a lot of

"It" Is God

ruminating over and we need to be patient there. %ere are secondary gains for some people that keep them hanging onto the same old same old. Check those out in your own life and others will become clearer. Poor me can be a way of life for some. Likely a learned behavior in their early life and hard to break. Ilinking is all that is needed to change, the perspective is everything and different for most.

Everything affects everything and has a rippling affect so when a solution does not come easy it is usually because something's are not in place yet. We really have a problem or challenge here. Patience are needed, harder for males in our culture than females. Many solutions are multi fascinate and therefore timing is everything. We are one and what effects one affects all. I liked it when the A-team said at the end of the program, "I like it when the plan came together". That is what we should wait for rather than pushing a solution. Perfect timing gives that peace that passes all understanding. You know when that happens and things are better than expected. Remember the universe wants to give you the desires of your heart.

I needed a sofa so neighbors and I went garage sale. There was one sofa but I did not settle for it. Tie last sale was an estate sale, the last of the day and there was my sofa. Perfect design, color and price. We were just so elated. Perfect timing and a witness for all of us on patience. So when prayers do not seem to get answered, tell yourself that the universe is working it all out to perfection. I call these high on life moments. Experiences are our teachers so therefore you learn to be more patient but it does take paying attention to life to know becoming is going on in your journey. Others may find your patience an issue but just keep on your own journey. No one knows where you are in our journey but you, so be comfortable in yourself. To live life is to be aware of where you are and that does bring contentment. We are in such a hurry to get the answers to challenges, we miss the opportunity to see or connect the dots of our adventures to make sense of life You do not have to work hard at it as it will just become a way of life. When I say I am going to pray, I am in prayer. When I say I am going to mediate, I am in mediation. When I say I am more aware I will be more aware. It is first a thought. Thinking is the powerhouse. Yes practice, practice does make it happen almost without much thought but desire is what is needed to start anything. Until you are aware of the experiences of being high on life it may sound like hocus pocus and you are not into it but once you experience it more is desired and understood. It takes just the effort of recognizing the coming together of everything. The more you recognize it the more it increases. See why it is important to be the living not the walking dead? Life just takes on a beautiful meaning and purpose. I believe if you ask 80% of Americans, what the purpose of life is that they would not have a realistic clue. That is sad for me. We should be taught early in life more about the purpose and the real meaning to life. Churches are failing to really do this but I do not believe they knew other than the taught doctrine. It maybe just the blind leading the blind. We are so primitive and even the early church was driven by economics. Not exactly something you want to take with you when you go home to heaven. If you did not know any better than you can see why you would not be judging yourself on it as you were unaware. It was a belief of the times, like a flat earth. If fact be known that most churches seem to be less concerned about life after death as they try to keep hold of power and control. If motive is not pure it will not last and as the bible say it will be eaten by moths or burn. Burn out! Controlling the masses is not that hard, just use fear. Fear is the opposite of love. You are going to hell when there is none. Remember there is no hell lest you make there one, so stop believing there is one. Who care who says there is one, you need to own your beliefs.

So what you take back to spirit world when you die is important not a necessity as you get many chances to get to where you need to go next. It is important however to know yourself and your connection to the universe. There are many universes so why this one and not another What are the major themes in your life as they tell you a lot about your purpose and meaning today. If the purpose of life is to become all you can become than seek and you shall find. Take this serious and the rewards will be exciting. This is the key to enjoying life and not wanting things to remain the same or fearing change. I see how much better off I was as a kid than they are today as I had to be creative with no electronics and technology to take away from the thinking. Technology is ok if we were not consumed by it. If a black out of technology happens tomorrow it will produce chaos. Systems just have no back up so lights, heat, banks, and everything else will be down. So fear will rein without a back up plan. This is bound to happen, so how is this progress? Did you ever hear of Atlantis? Well it was a culture that was far advanced from ours and they too had advanced technology that advanced beyond their knowledge of how to balance it and it destroyed them. Are we heading there? We do seem to be backing ourselves into a corner. and it is driven by economics. We will spend money here but not there as in education not enough, war to much, insurance, and medicine running our lives with fear and many issues that are not seen by some as important when they should be priorities. God fearing peoples, when some never think of God except when tragedy strikes. Isn't it a contradiction to want power and control and being Godly? Many of those in power and control fail to see we are all one and when we go down they will too. In the crash of the thirties it was the wealthy that jumped off bridges. Their identity being with money. We have not recovered from the '08 recession and we are headed for another as the middle class got the picture but those that were in power did not. Money is going to become valueless as it is over in flatted now. The solutions are ones that no one wants to deal with as it is so far reaching into everything but inevitable. No nice way out of a bad created situation. The adjustment after wars are always problematic. Now with our first female president it will not be an easy start but the female touch will be more likely to make the medicine go down better. Obama will be a great help to her. Tie Blacks will fair better than the rest as they know how to tough it out by history. This thinking is just common sense. The power and control today see themselves as insolated from it all as they are blind or believe it cannot happen to them. Now this is not all bad as it will help us move into the next phase of our development, which is community. It will take us all to put life back on track. Not the same old but new direction.

Female/male balance of power. It is too bad that disaster has to change our course but that is not new. History does repeat itself as we are slow to learn. Terms in office will be seen as necessary to help this from happening again.

Thereal issue is that those that see themselves in power never want to give it up and the longer they are in office the more entrenched they become. It is dangerous as we will now see.

You are a unique important individual and how you experience situation is different than the next person. So paying attention to experiences and what they are all about instead of just having them is key to life. What happened with the good old boys society was they never really helped each other grow. They put a blind eye to the corruption until on outsider exposed it. In these troubled times there is a lot of exposure and much more to come.

Enlightenment is the process of knowing and needs attention. Thlis is not all laboring attention. It is just reflecting on the situation especially those that keep happening to you.

Take a moment to think, why do I have this experience over and over with the same results. If you had siblings and asked them to recall an experience that you had with them and they do not remember it, that was something that was for you not them. You are in your own journey as they are. Experiences are our teachers if we are willing to learn. We get revelations today as we did in days of old "It"/God speaks to us as "it" always has. But who is listening? "It" is that still small voice. My sheep will know my voice. Do you? If not just be persistent and ask and you will receive. You cannot fool mother nature or God so be ready. Remember "It" is an energy not a person so stop giving "It" emotions, only feelings. God is warm and fuzzy for me with a good sense of humor as well as playfulness.

To know God is to love God and know God as love. To know God is to have a relationship with God. I believe that I was born with a strong sense of God as my relationship seems to have no beginning or end. It is awesome but do not think life is easy because of it. To whom I give much much is expected and my trails and tribulation have been intents. The fine tuning of life does not seem to get easier but you feel less alone.

Following the dots become clearer as you get older and that is why I like to call life a journey. You are traveling from one experience to another with purpose and meaning as to what you want to be. Hopefully more God like.

Experiences are our teachers if we are willing to learn. Each experience unique to each individual because we are all learning differently for different reasons. That is why it is important to be about our own tasks and not comparing it to the others. No comparison, no right/wrong or good/ bad. There is a whole picture that we are not privileged to yet. I for years used an analogy of a puzzle to understand my growth as putting a puzzle together one piece at a time kept me looking at what I had, what I knew and what was missing. It helped me with patience as well as knowing that more was to come. Until the last piece was put in place I did not have the full picture It is the game of life. Patience, awareness, and vigilant are all part of the process to enlightenment. definition of enlightenment is to be free of ignorance, prejudice and to be informed. It is a beautiful word. Ignorance just means not knowing. We culturally use words as negative when they are neutral. Ignorance has little to do with intelligent. The bible says that there is so much knowledge that there are not enough libraries to hold it all. So you and I will never know much and that is good news as it would be boring if there was nothing to learn. We strive more for money and survival than anything else. Survival being the lowest rung in the ladder of life and that is why we are a primitive. If a majority in our culture are just surviving than it effects all of us. The unrest in our country today is not there because some part of our population is bad but because of the unequalness. We would do well to listen to them but powers to be are not willing too. We are primitive because we are in the blaming game and that is keeping us dead in the water. You cannot go forward if you blame or want to focus on blame. That is why forgiveness is so important. Forgive to move on.

Technology has advanced (?) so fast that we do not know what to do if it all goes amuck and how to dispose of the old or waste products in manufacturing. Our solutions are to send the old to undeveloped and unaware countries.

We are adolescence at our best and we do not take time to figure out consequences of our behavior until it is too late. It is all about economics and competition. Do we really need a new version of the old? The old was just fine and where do you draw the line? I have windows 10 and it sets there useless to me. I am using XP version for writing this book and all programs rebel against me using it. We are being forced to buy new. Does anyone care until it is too late?

As long as we focus on money and competition we are missing the meaning of life as you cannot take it with you when you go home to spirit world. How many times have you heard someone who is dying, wish that they could give all their money for a longer healthier life when their focus was success and money? We all need to focus on what is important in life and of value. Don't sweat the small stuff as it is all small stuff except that which you take with you to spirit world, which is energy; your beliefs and thoughts are energy. Spirit, soul, essence, aura, God, "It" are all energy. So your energy is the most important part of you and hopefully the part you spent more time and attention too from now on. Everything we do is a choice. So everything is positive if we choose it to be. That is a learning growing experience. So choose to be upbeat about life and see what is happening.

One day I decided to smile and say hi to everyone I met and see what happened. At the end of the day I really felt good and most of the people I said hi to acknowledge me. I had a feeling of accomplishment as it was not my usual style. If one person was made to feel better about the day than that was an accomplishment. I did feel that other like the recognition. We are in our own little world most of the time so could do that everyday but likely do not. Try something for yourself and see what happens as you challenge your Being. Starting somewhere can open a new direction for you. My daughter came home from college one day and said she had started a rumor about herself to see how long it took for it to get back to her. I said, "you did not" but she had. She had a hard time fitting into the world of craziness. If you are bored with your life step out of your comfort zone and take a risk. I had this nice little sign in my office that was titled, "Risk" and it basically stated if you were not taking any then you were not going anywhere. I am in the biggest risk of my life right now and it is not easy to believe it will turn out just fine when there is no sign that it will. I will let you know how it turns out. Tiere is no right or wrong place to start. Choosing to change our behavior is always going to be a struggle but usually worth it. The struggle is the old fighting with the new. Testing is part of it all as just when you think it is behind you it pops up as a trail again. The universe/God wants to make sure you have really changed your beliefs. Telling other what you are doing also is usually helpful as they can be encouraging and supportive. That is why groups like weight watchers, exercise, and therapy groups work for some. You are less likely to feel alone in the struggle If you say you are bored, watch out as something will pop up to challenge you. You may think you did not ask for it but you likely did. Follow it as it will lead you to where you need to go and for the most part it will be better than you thought. Remember the universe wants to give you the desires of your heart. "It" is for you not against you for it would have to be against itself. It is not desirable to skip to many understandings in acquiring the desires of your heart, as each step helps you to really understand and change you beliefs and behavior. This idea always takes me back to why Jesus got angry at his followers for wanting more and more miracles. If too many miracles than the steps to understanding is lost.

If you are a parent then you know that teaching your child is a process of successions or age appropriate teachings. I stayed home for 19 years to raise my children.

These writings are really a lot of my experiences and sort of a short version of my autobiography.

I read everything I could find about parenting. I sometimes got the information I needed just days before needing it. It was awesome. It was a lesson on getting what you needed just in time. I first had to have the desire to be the best possible parent I could be. That was the desire of my heart. My parents were awesome and a good example for me for they were unselfish. The universe knew what I desired so gave me what I needed to do just that. I had given up a job I loved with Eastern Air Lines and married so went pell mell into my job of parenting. If asked what I did I said, "I have the best job, I'm a Mom" I said this so much that my son said one day "but Mom no one says that "But I loved my job. I later had a job for 30 years that I also loved as a psychotherapist. The strange part of both jobs was that I never set out to be a parent or psychotherapist. I believe they chose me and were a perfect fit for my personality. I always do everything with gusto. I am now cleaning out my attic to move and it tells my story very well as I have 9 suitcases for travel, 6 pair of skies for cross country and downhill skiing, 8 pair ice skates, 6 pair roller blades and too many golf clubs to count. I also have my original, bought at 19, roller skates. Do I horde, not me! All my activities were with exercise in mine. Staying physically fit was the need behind these activities. I have always taken a holistic approach to life. body, mind and spirit.

I believe I died giving birth to my first son and that might be the reason for my big joy at being a Mom I had an out of body experience and do not remember much for six hours. My husband thought that I had died also as no one would tell him why he saw his son but not his wife. I was bleeding to death and being worked on and had no pulse as when I came around I heard a delighted intern say he had gotten a pulse and shortly later I was being asked to tell them the time. The clock was right ahead of me and it was 9:30am and my son was born at 3:20am. I was told by the doctor that he was going to give me a blood transfusion and later said he was not. I believe my son was born unassisted as remember back then you were placed in a curtained cubby hole of a room and according to the doctor in the birth it had torn everything wanting to get out but now I needed to drink lots of fluid. My husband was not happy until I drank a quart of fluid when he was there until I was leaking so much milk that the doctor said, Did not anyone tell you to stop drinking so much" and they had not. Now I had the best doctor of the day and When I was sent back to planet earth that things for me were anew and my purpose in life were much more pronounced. I am also a Sagittarius so make lemonade out of lemons. It was of course never talked about back then so it wasn't until years later that I had another out of body experience that I started on my quest to understand the unknown spiritual worlds. A wonderful quest. Being a reader I started to read about human behavior, God/spirit, history, and psychology. It was pretty much an alone quest. My church was very much in my life but of little help in it all.

A good friend, a writer said that everyone should do their autobiography as no one knows your story but you. My sons will be surprised to read some of this too. This is the only way I could get a autobiography going as I tried but it just did not go well.

God has always been strong in my life and I was never passive in it all. Even as a 7 and 8 year old young girl, leaving my body each night through a vortex I made is very vivid for me today. My quest for the unknown was strong but much of the time quietly done. And over the years I had many spiritual experiences. There is still more unknown than known. Five years ago I met a psychic group who were studying all those phenomena that I had known from the bible but no one talked much about. Churches seemed to be threaten by the unknown as it took them out of control and power over. I am a self healer and have been for 40 years so I attended a class at our local BOCES on reiki, an old Japanese healing. I paid the $90. to see who would attend as I live in such a backward community That is my observation as a psychotherapist from day one of my 30 years there but no better place for me to grow and get stronger than being isolated in my beliefs. Now

15 people attended which was very surprising for me. They were nurses, teachers, and a couple from this psychic group. That is how I started to attend the groups and met delightful people. I had found the others! Now this town I lived in had a military base and for sometime I refused to see military families as you will never meet a more anti militant person than me as for me war is barbaric and primitive. I was sought out and finally got certified for the military only to find out that we had more in common than I though as their spirituality was more to my beliefs. Just a note here if you are faced with death and dying everyday than your belief system needs to be strong and I found them having the unconventional beliefs more in line with mine. God works in mysterious ways. Lois had found the others.

It is a good lesson in you get what you need when you need it not before or after. We are all in different places in our journey and it is important to realize that, so we do not compare our journey with others.

Like minded people are what keeps us stuck or can enhance our growth. We need to know when to move away or when to embrace. I needed to embrace so to not feel alone. It was time for the others. My love for God was connected to the churches, so was hard to break away. I was raised Methodist from my Mother's side. Coming to America in 1629, they were Quakers/Pilgrims. Most of my life in growing up I lived in a Catholic neighborhood. Back then the Catholic church in my hometown taught that Protestants went to hell which there is none. My prayers each night were four prayers which two were Catholic prayers. I always ended my prayers with, "And God I know you are the God of the Protestants too". I said this from probably 7 to 19 years of age. Since my friends were Catholic, I attended the church with them but they could not go to mine. All of this seems so funny today but it is an example of how our beliefs define us and how wrong they can be. I feel blessed today for that upbringing as it gave me strength.

Now God does not have favorites in any religions and there is no hell or devil. Why would there be? Man want the so called BAD to get theirs. Well it tells us not to judge. A local church just put on their outside billboard, "Jesus is God and Ali is the devil". Now where is Christ in that? This minister is blind to the fact that there is no Christ in that. God does not need us to defend him. We are all created by God and All God's children. Love your neighbor as your self. Lots of fear in this minister not love. Now this is my observation. God is unconditional love, please get this. No favorites. At 4 years old the thing I loves the most about church was the hymn, "That Jesus loves me this I know for the Bible tells me so . That does not state an exclusive belief for it says me. If you are not showing love you are showing fear. We do not seem to have even a basic teachings of Christ down yet. We have been stuck in arguing history rather than the teaching and example he gave us. They are the only lasting importance. If Jesus came again what would it be called? reincarnated Jesus So as the decuples you already believe in reincarnation, you are just stuck in the taught word.

Over the years I have asked Catholics in other parts of the world if they were taught that Protestants went to hell and some said yes and some said no. The only reason for the teaching was fear. I believe my sister who is a convert to Catholism is still stuck in most of these beliefs. The sad thing is that everyone wants to be important so to be important they have something others do not but want. It set up an unfavorable mind set that can be very destructive of true character So finding self is more difficult as they already have it. If you think you have it you are not going to develop new ideas and you protect what is.

Now I am not the authority on anything but I have read the Bible cover to cover five times, studied it for 17 years. Read the Book of Mormon's, the Koran, some Torah and countless others as I felt that if I did not know this I could not know why I believed that. Why do I believe what I do? Because likely some human told me it was so. Now 1 and 1 are still two or is it? Uno plus uno is dos. or is it? So are we caught up in a word rather than taking back the word for it's other meanings. Evolution is one of the word that confuse people more than not because of the religious take on the word.

You are evolving like it or not. You avoid the word out of ignorance. Do not throw the baby out with the bath water. Darwin was not all wrong so if you have problems with some part of his concepts do not discard it all. A lot of churches are all in nothing thinkers. How many of them want you to challenge their beliefs? Open mouth and swallow that is it?

Stop being led and own your beliefs. Of course if you got this far in these writings you are more open than likely most. So what is the difference in my telling you something here than any other source? No different as here too you need to take away only what rings true for you. Remember the puzzle is only ready for the next piece as you made it so. So take away only what fits you or what I like to say rings true for you.

Here is an exercise: for three months take the time you would spend in rituals of beliefs and question each belief about God that you have and see what happens because I contend that we just do not think or take the time to look at them. See what happens. God says test and try me. Now tell God that is your intent. "It" has a lot of humor as I am a doubting Thomas and test and try everything through the firry furnace before I change my beliefs. How I did the testing and trying was by more and more research, meaning more reading and studying. You say you do not have time, well I went to bed early and read, or when waiting in line for something like doctors office or today on the phone, just squeeze it in and if you were like me, isolate yourself after a while as it became fun, exciting and a good drive. I found that I was best in the early morning so most of these writings were done from 3am to 6am. Do you know why I think I am more receptive in these hours? You are likely thinking she going to tell us anyway!! OK it is because after rest I am more open and flesh is more likely out of the way for the reception. Remember flesh is ego. I really see it as my revelation time. So our experiences are our teachers. It is not that we never have the truth it is that everything is evolving. It is hard for me to think that we do not know God after all this time and why "It" is really needed so we move ahead with our concept of God as spirit, energy or soul. God is not human and never needed to be but does understand humanness.

"It" Is God

I have for years awaken at about 3am with what I called sermons in my head. I did try to write them down either then or later but I did find later not so good. If you do not want to get up and write them down lay there for a minute and reflect on them so to put them in long term memory. Reflecting and rehearsing are the techniques we use to transfer short term memory to long or learned memory.

Example: At the time of my divorce in the late 70's I threw a lot of tantrums as I was hearing that I was not going with my then husband on his new adventure. I did not believe in divorce so kept telling God that the voice could not be "It". God was very patience with me. I learned a lot from the whole experience as it has been worth all of the heartaches. I loved my husband but we were not good for each other, more me than him as I cannot speak for him. I had stopped being me and was this lamb to slaughter as a lot of women were at this time. Good wife, good mother, good church goers, and a people pleaser. You cannot regret what you were as you did not know any better. I was free to find me again and boy going from middle class to poverty was not easy but you have some very important lessons to learn and there is no other way but the road of hard knocks. Now I was a very independent gal before marriage and worked for a job I loved with Eastern Air Lines but dropped the me for a new roll of wife and Mom. No regrets as today I see that I would never gone where I needed to go if I had kept that identity. I am still a people pleaser but know when it is harmful and when it isn't. This experience helped me be a better psychotherapist as even a victim can learn to be a survivor. You usually learn that you were the reason for the lesson. Not deserve it but the experience has good lessons in it. I was sexually abused as a child but became sex therapist and taught Human Sexuality in college, not to make sex bad or negative but help clients see survival and sexuality as a gift from God. "It"/God made us sexual 365 days a year and no accident, a beautiful aspect of humanness Sex is not good in our universe as it was power over for too long. Women are taking back their rights and having say in it all. Long time coming. No one gives us the easy road because we would not learn from it. No pain no gain. Survival takes forgiveness as the first step, not approving the act but not letting the act define you for the rest of your life. If no forgiveness than the act still has power over. I am saddened when people do not forgive for years if ever for their losses. Do I reflect on my daughters death in desire to have her here or needing her input today, yes but it is short lived as she is with me in spirit and I know her presence. Try to get this! One morning I had showered and was toweling off when I saw this green suave on my tummy, now it was like a lipstick substance, looked at my towel and none on it, looked around the room nothing green in sight. Next thought Christine, my daughter. Now I wrapped this substance off with toilet paper and a tissue. Still have it. Now one son is a hydro geologist and has a lot of samples tested in labs for substance. Called him to see if he could have a lab test this sample but before I called him I all ready knew it was a substance that would be unknown. Remember I am a doubting Thomas so my son called two labs. One said it would be very expensive and the other said it would likely not be enough to test. Now I am smart enough to know that both were not good answers BUT they were the answers I was to have. Know when to hold them and know when to let them go. I just laughed because I already knew. My daughter was laughing too. There as more mysteries to this world than not. In spirit terms my daughter cannot, not be a part of me. "Test and try me" is a standard for me and there is no shame in that.

God experiences life through us. We are all one. Being emotional is a human trait. We can do without emotions so to make decisions better and from a higher place, a clear mind. Not judged by the past or future but of the now. Staying in present moment. Emotions are created from our past experiences so cloud the present day decisions. Staying in the Now is operating in the present day mode and not the past is usually making a different decision than you would have in the past moving you out of your comfort zone and into new growth. Without emotions we will likely be more realistic and fresh. This sometime has a spiritual feeling to it and seems like other than you made the decision. It maybe a foreign feeling to you at first but it is likely the presents of God that you are experiencing. It can be a high on life with fear as you want to take the decision back and return to same old safety net. Go with the high on life and see where it goes. You have let go of ego and are making the decision from your pure essence. The essence of you is why God did not make junk. The core of you is pure love like God is unconditional love. If only everyone sensed and felt this in an unselfish act. We would then experience and know God. God does not hide from us nor does "It" want us to fear God. As a child of God, "It" wants me to experience unconditional love as well as to give unconditional love. My children were my teachers in unconditional love as they let me know in a respectful way, when I was not being unconditional love and was conditional love. It was actually cute as out of the mouth of babes come much honesty and wisdom until we squash it. In higher evolved civilizations it is not squashed but encouraged.

All this teaching helped me be a better psychotherapist as I could not be effective if I was judgmental. Each of us has a different journey for different reasons. Depression to me is the lack of action in your life and only you know what will change that. Hopelessness is sometimes the root of our lack of insight. God wants to give you the desires of your heart so what is it that you desire. Many people believe they are not worthy of the desires of their heart and that comes much of the time from religion. Never good enough. Fear again keeps us from moving forward and we should look at the unknown with excitement. Fear of making mistakes is at the root of change. We need to be more adventurous. Take back the power of your thinking.

Rehearse your new thinking by saying it over and over until you believe it. God loves me, God loves me and I know God loves me. I have all I need within. If it does not hurt yourself, others, or property than go for it. Looking for approval from others keeps us from moving forward. So start not caring where the others are unless they are where you want to be then you can use them to find out how to get to where you now want to go. It might look like this: If they can do it than I can. I learned to scuba dive at 62, the oldest in the class. Wonderful instructor who paired me up with the youngest in the class, his 9 year old niece. The niece made me a kid again and I let go of all inhibitions. Brilliant move as I am not even a good swimmer but if it can be learned than it is possible for all. I have 17 open dives but know at 77 it is not advisable for me to go any more. Like outer space it is hard on the body.

It is an awesome experience to live in the now and be open to whatever come next instead of projecting from the past experiences or future fears. You might say, you got the experience of being God. The God in you. It is there to be discovered. The meaning of life is to become all you can become and that is God like. I wish I could just give this to everyone but it would take away from the process of learning and owning the experience. Remember Jesus did not want you to get accustom to miracles as took away the process of knowing.

After years of isolation and asking for people on my page to relate too, as I said I found a group besides those I found in the books I read. When you feel alone it is easy to forget God is always there and never leave you. But I do know my alone times had great value. First I was busy with my career and it took at lot of my energy. Secondly, it gave me time to read and study. Next it gave me time to mediate and talk to God. Knowing is important in order to see the bigger picture and most of the time it helped me move to a more positive picture. My feeling are a choice so thinking changes my feeling to a better place. Mind games? Yes it is but if it is all a choice than I choose to feel good over feeling alone, sad, depressed, or any feeling that brings me down. Being honest with yourself is one of the first lessons to learn in growth and development. It is so easy to fool ourselves into justifying our feelings and staying on the pity pot or poor me phase. One practice I started was I stopped laughing at jokes I did not get and just said I did not get them. I am still a little late at getting some. You learn much more by being honest with the little things. As a psychotherapist clarification is of major importance as with the English language words have different meaning to different people. Six year olds were cute as when asking them for clarification because they spoke a different language, (youth vs. aged) their eyes would get big and the attention was keen as now I needed something from them. Everyone wants to be heard and tell their story. You can learn a lot from a six year old. Language is the most misunderstood in our ways to communicate. So we all need to be comfortable with clarification. So not understanding something does not take away from your intelligent but could add to it.

You cannot learn something if you are pretending to know it but is alright not to want to know something so do not engage. any further. As time goes on the knowing when or when not to engage becomes freedom, no right or wrong but a choice. You see your responsibility for your choices and many things just naturally fall away with no interest in them anymore. The worldly things pass away and the spiritual things increase. It is not likely a struggle as it is a choice both consciously and unconsciously. Your unconscious now knows that you are serious, also the universe knows and God knows. Interests just change and so may direction but that should be examined carefully before doing especially if it is a direction never though of before. It just might be emotional and not a sound. choice. Emotional decisions may be made only to be regretted later. Some people have given up everything not needing worldly things only to find themselves with a divorce, no job or income and just a shock to the system Sleep on these decisions and see if you feel the same after awhile. Sometimes it is just the wrong time in life to start over with ideal directions. There is no urgency in God or spirit. Making major decisions should be done with research and all family members as that will make for a check and balance system for the decision. Risks need to be taken in order to grow but with intelligence. God is more likely to be common sense than not. The universe is order; cause and effect, natural laws are in place and this is common sense. Unleash a though, idea, or situation and it than effects the energy of all. When you say, "what goes around comes around" you are saying that the action that was unleashed is now in motion. It is not that the energy could not be diverted but that the action to divert is not taken due to the person now responsible is not thinking of the consequences or is in full belief that it will not happen to them. Consequences are not one of our strong suits culturally.

Logic is taught at the college level but not many take it as it is thought to be for science and not everyday use when everyone could benefit from using logic.

I stayed home for 19 year to raise my children and it afforded me with the time and energy to help them with reasoning. I have always been a thinker. Friends say to much in my head but when it is balanced it works well.

My children grew up on Long Island for the most part and in a mixed Christian/Jewish neighborhood. which was a good combination. When my oldest was going to be 13 and his friends were also. The boy next door was Jewish and we as parents were preparing them for the rights of passage. I was dropping my son off at church for confirmation and John's mom and dad were going to the synagogue to learn how to let go of their children and help them with decision making. At least that is what I got out of my conversation with John's Mom as to why parent attend classes at this time in their children's life. I liked the idea and shared it with the children so we were on the same page. It is a valuable teaching. Christians I felt were at a disadvantage at this point. Helping teens take responsibility for decision making at this age is the most valuable lesson we can give them. I talked to my minister about this and he said he agreed but could not see Christian parent ready for it. I am glad for this teaching as my children seem to benefit also. In this teaching is the lesson of responsibility for decision and actions. I never took parenting lightly and if you teach respect and responsibility as well as show it things just go better. My parents demanded both from us and I am glad. It seems to have gone out of fashion today and look around and see how hard it is for teens today to have good direction. What is needed is less sports and more family time. Mom does not have to give up a career just less trucking children to .this or that. The 40 to 60 year old seem lost in our culture today and they have raised our young adults. The children are not to blame but it is easy to blame them.

Accountability and responsibility are lost and anything goes as long as you can get away with it. It is only a lie if you get caught otherwise it is a cleaver move. We are seeing more and more exposure of corruption and it will get worse before it get better. The good old boys society is finally breaking down and the interesting part is that as women come into power we will more balance along with honesty and openness.

The male ego has gone unchecked for to long in our culture which was primarily cause by the male dominate church teachings. God was distorted and left unchecked. for far too long in a male dominate belief. Now many today still want it back to male dominance but it is not in God's plan. How do I know because he told me so. This is why it is very important to speak out about the distortions and misconceptions. Many have been silent for too long. Many have fallen away from the church in the past ten years knowing that God was unconditional love and it was missing from the actions of most Christians lives. The church became a habit or social with little substances that was pertinent for today's life. It was basically history and not even good history. Unconditional love does not create an unbalance of powers. Why would it? Look around Spring follows Winter and so forth. Tie walking dead society does not question concepts as it is comfortable keeping the status quo. Maybe in their defense they are chasing the wrong meaning of life; fame, fortune, and ego. None of them are of any value as unconditional love is energy not material. Mind over matter. Unconditional love is at the heart of it all and is God. "It" would not be unconditional love if it had favorites, chosen people, sexual preference, color of skin and etc.

Recently a female announced to me that she could not believe in the God of present day popular beliefs. She was surprised by my response that she "well should not." Within a short conservation she felt relief that she and I were on the right page for us and it has sound biblical backing. It all depends on where you are in your search and interpretation. Go for your truth and stop thinking someone else has the answers for you. Now I do believe you will need to read the Bible cover to cover and have a personal relationship with God. That is know "It's" voice, that still small voice. Remembering God meets you where you are at. So if you believe that that stone will produce water, it will produce water. I over the years have had thing happen that will not work today as I am in a different place in my walk with God. If thing are happening the same today for you as long ago that might mean that you are stuck. No right or wrong it just is. Seek and you will find, ask and it will be given unto you, a new revelation to get you excited again and searching. You are not on planet earth to get stale or comfortable. I cannot go back to some of my old beliefs than fly and they seem silly that I ever believed them in the first place. In a sense I never believed them in the first place, I am just remembering the higher belief again. Why do we forget what we knew in spirit world? Well to remember again is the joy and heaven on earth of life. Ihe living a "God" life. Remember all of heaven sings when we remember and that reaches us in the high in life experiences. We are remembering and it is such a joy and a revelation to uncover more of the truth. Right now I am hearing the song in my head, "In the Garden", and "It" walks with me and "It" talks with me in the garden. Now I am crying, not me crying but my spirit. See my spirit is so happy that I listen to that still small voice and that I am willing to share it with you. Discovering the joys of life and one size does not fit all nor should it. We fail to realize that our journeys are not the same nor for the same reasons as we came to planet earth for different reasons. So why tell my story? Well it is likely more therapeutic for me in recapping my journey than not but it might just help others relate. It is hard to relate if you have not experienced some of it as a personal journey.

In AA there is a step that says, "do not take others inventory". If we would be sure to take our own inventory only, what a different world we would have and such freedom for all. Free to be me the real quest of human life. Our beliefs and culture would be totally different; no wars, no competing except with self, no right or wrong, no good or bad. The competing with self only to improve and advance our BEING. Life would be more exciting and less destructive. Discovering this is freedom, joy, and love with a whole new set of beliefs and decision making skills. Decisions making skills that are unselfish and more fair for everyone. Equal opportunity would be a natural with no need to fight for it. Differentness would be seen as beauty and inspiring. Do you really think God created us the way "It" did by mistake? Check to see if you act as if God did not know what it was doing or is everything just random?

If God created you? Didn't God create the black, white, yellow, red, gay, lesbian, transgender and all other characteristics. It was all in the plan. My gay friends say to me, "can you imagine someone in our culture choosing to be gay? So many tried not to be and it did not work. Now do not tell me that Sodom and Gomorrah was about homosexuality as it about disobedience. Read it again. So many contradictions in our beliefs.

Did I have a part in the script for my life this time around? If I did maybe I chose to be healthy and became a self-healer out of the necessity of proving that it is all in the mind and that God never intended us to be sick so refuse it. You bring to you what you believe. So in really believing this my immune system developed so every cell in my body now knows that I know we were not created to be sick and it is in the mind. This idea was created by my higher power and did not happen over night. It has been over 40 years in the making and it took a series of events as proof. I had to be aware and alert to these events in order to recognize them God said test and try me and I did just that to bring them about as solid beliefs. If I created them it is still God creating as God and I are one. God is in me. You and I are one if you believe that God is in you. This is the part that the church squashed or did not do well in helping us to understand. It is all in the Bible It is about you being it, feeling it and understanding it. Churches for me had no clue of how to get you to understand how God is in you but Jesus said, "That God and I are one". How are you to know that but by the process of dissecting your beliefs. You cannot say one thing and act another. Most Christians are not knowing or following Christ beliefs and this is so disturbing for me. If you call yourself a Christian and do not study for yourself what and who Jesus was so how can you be Christ like. Know the difference in using the word Jesus and Christ. They are different concepts and Christ in you is not the same as Jesus in you. Go back in history and see the difference. Second clue!

Jesus accepted all and because we still want to be special, we do not even accept all in Christ. How dare us not to see everyone as special and God's design. Jesus' followers were mostly women but his disciples were men due to the Jewish traditions. Women support the church today as did in old. God is more with feminine traits than not. Women are more about change than men as women need less control of situations than males in our culture and are willing to try new ideas. It is still more women in the Spiritual movement than men as we try to find our way back to God. Dan Brown's book "The Da Vinci Code" was a best seller because many people are looking for less contradictions and the truth in the teachings of God.

The biggest contradiction is unconditional love. My children helped me see my contradictions in unconditional love. When a parent tells a child that what they did was not good enough, that is conditional love. Now unconditional love would ask if that was the best they could do and go from the answer given.

The person already knows if they did their best now you need to know. Unconditional love does not come from your needs but from theirs. This is where God get blamed for our lack of awareness. God is doing nothing to us. We do it to ourselves. Wrong decisions, next learning or remembering, a desire for change both known or unknown, and help on our journey. Most religions tell us we are not good enough.

Reading the Bible cover to cover helps you see the need for experiences to change the present thinking of the period. Not that the thinking was to stay stagnant as we have done today. History is important for this reason to help us see where we have been and not to stay there but be creative. Creativity, a wonderful gift.

Hell and the devil are only real if you make them so. So why make them so? You are what you believe. So work on the belief that there is no hell or devil before you die as you take with you what you believe. Also work on you are good enough. God does not make junk as you are make perfect and all you have to do is peel away the layers to find the self that is authentically you. Not the ego self but the real you. Free to be you and me.

Everyone might start by define success as it is different for everyone as our journey is different. Success is not what culturally we think it is but is individualized. The person born in poverty and remains in poverty could be very successful in accepting their walk of life and be doing what was intended for their journey. Why? Because accepting what is can be the greatest relief one can have instead of being a Wantabee, which culturally we are driven to be. Excepting ones lot in life maybe a strong point in character. Building character is far more important than money. You can take that with you when you go. Peace of mind is very valuable. Imagine being worry free for life and how that affects life. Worry being the biggest waste of energy for the mind. Three forth of our worries never come true and therefore we worry for nothing. As I have said before there are women that think worry is a sign of love when it is a lack of trust. Trusting that you will know what you need too know about the situation in due time and trusting them to come out alright helps them to do that. You bring to you what you believe. Everything will be alright and it usually is.

Fear of making mistakes or having to handle the mistakes of others is a strong root of worry. My definition for mistakes is that they are learning growing experiences so therefore I do not make mistakes but have learning growing experiences. If your religion used a lot of fear of God rather than the love of God than you have either panic attacks or your never good enough to see or know God. Fear based religions are still prevalent today. Parenting based on fear is not good parenting either. Yet we have kids that fear is the reason they do the right thing to please the parent. Far better that the child is taught why they should do this not that. It teaches consequences. You do not need to earn love from anyone or thing but you do earn respect. Unconditional love does not say, "I will love you when". This is so important in knowing God. Check to see where you are in your beliefs and if you are good enough. Not good enough when but now.

Having read all or part of the books of world religions including the Bible, Torah, Koran, Taoism, and Buddhism I saw that all religions are about unconditional love and knowing God in you. Your potential not someone else's. Buddha tried to get his disciples to look at Buddhism as a way of life not a religion but we all want it to be a religion. Christianity is based a lot in Buddhism as is Judaism. Jesus tried to teach a way of life not rules and regulations. Buddhism is very positive and beautiful. lhe Bible can be seen as very negative, angry God, not good enough and God having favorites. There are no favorites on earth or in heaven for God. We are all God's children and as I have said before if God had favorites that would not be unconditional love. Because Jesus was Jewish the early churches used his heritage to produce a favorite peoples. It became a religion in itself and stops Christianity from moving ahead. The spirit of Jesus has to be very astounded at where his teaching have gone. They have become so grossly distorted for personal gain and monitory gain. Jesus' teachings are all that is important not his birth or humanness.

Jesus came to planet earth to change some teachings of the time as the Sadducee who only accepted the written laws and the Pharisee, who accepted the written laws as well as oral laws were teaching some ungodly ideas. The Pharisee's were very self-righteous and powerful. Jesus was a prophet Power over was an issue then and it is today.

God sends messengers all the time to help us move ahead but who is lessening? Mostly those who are already on the road of enlightenment as the rest think they have arrived already. If you are stuck in a punitive God image than you likely had a rough relationship with your Dad so it is hard to see unconditional love. Having taught parenting skills it is hard for some parents to let go of punitive techniques as it may have worked for them with their parents. Reasoning from day one with children is rewarding but do not over due that either as it can become too authoritarian. Lesson to them.

"It" Is God

Human's seems to have a need throughout history to be special and important and religion was no exception. There is no sainthood here or in heaven. Much of our violence today has it's root cause in the lack of recognition and being heard. Unequalness based on economics is the sin. Remember the rich man likely will have a harder time getting into heaven. Why? Because of how he got his money and what he did with it. Money is not the problem but the use of money can be.

Attitude is everything. Thinking is the powerhouse. This is why I believe if you are a negative person, you can chip away at the negativity and become more positive. You can arrive at a loving God who has no favorites, you are good enough already, and working with unconditional love, than life becomes about the good life. If you believe that you scripted your life and purpose for coming to planet earth than you know you can get through whatever you are facing. You do not have to like it, just find a way beyond it knowing it has some revelations in it for you. One of my client had read Betty Eddie's book, "Embraced By the Light", and said she now felt she could get through all her trials. That is the power of beliefs. A bumper sticker once said, God does not give you more than you can handle, it just seems at times "It" does. Read also, "Why Bad Tling Happen to Good People." and "Don't Sweat The Small Stuff, It Is All Small Stuff".

These title alone say it all and are inspiring. When in the mist of feeling this is the worse case scenario you have ever been through, stop and look back and realize you have come through a lot of rough times and are better for them. When I have three things happen to me in a row, I ask for the fourth and it always makes me laugh. Three is enough and the fourth is funny. Lighten up and it helps too. Negativity brings negativity. This is why it is important to look at life as a path or journey for it can remind you that it all has positive meaning. Ask the situation, "What is it trying to teach me" The situation is now a living energy and everything is energy. God is energy.

We like to stay in the comfort zone but learning takes place out of our comfort zone. If we do not take risks we are not going anywhere. Go back to what you think success is and if it is anything other than growing and expounding upon your already knowing than is not increased your gifts or ability. What makes a differences in this life time is how we have increased our knowing since it is all we take with us to spirit world. Fame and fortune only translate by what we did with those gifts. What have you done to increase each gift you were given? We evolve culturally very slowly because we do not understand the meaning of life is to become all you can become. We could all be millionaires if we wanted to put the time and effort into that. It is not luck, education or by chance. except at the casinos.

I took at friend to a casino and gave her a dollar to put in the penny machine and she asked what the strategy to win was and I said it was all by chance. Her remark than why do it. Good point as many have found they gain nothing from get rich quick schemes, in fact it can ruin their life's path. When you earn it the hard way you are learning as you go alone the steps in handling the increase. One church got away with gambling for years because it was a church. It was called bingo but it was still gambling. When money is involved it is gambling. Gambling meaning chance. Getting rich quick is not a healthy desire.

Our focus is on fame and fortune when it is better to focus on spirit than matter. There is more than the body there is the essence, spirit, energy, mind, and things not seen or understood to seek after. We are not encouraged to seek after these things enough. The mysteries of life are far more exciting as everything else is fleeting and the moths can devour them.

Let's look at war and what it does and doesn't do. It is first primitive, barbaric, adolescence, and uncivilized. So how far have we come? You can remember our history by it's wars. Most wars gain nothing and some can have some value. Religion is the center of most of them or at least used to justify them. So we could conclude that God is important to most peoples one way or another. We still seem to have my God is better than your God even though we say we are all one with one God. Flhat is primitive.

"It" Is God

Now how would an advanced civilization settle disputes? Through negotiations. Adolescence does not look ahead at the consequences of behavior therefore cause much grief and pain as war does the same and no one really wins. The United States had a civil war and we are still adjusting to it 150 years later due to the pain and grief of it all. It was fought over the non accepting of one sector of God's creation.

Negotiation is about a give and take concept. No winning or losing but a fair agreement for all. Religion has not been of much help here and as said before there is no separation between church and state. If we are in war, where is the separation if it is about religious beliefs being different. We can say beliefs caused the wars. Beliefs are thoughts and not in a vacuum but out there. When beliefs are thought of mine is better than yours, where is God? We are all "It's" children and made us all. Why? Differences is the beauty and help us define who and what we want to be. Accept everyone but choose who you will follow. My beliefs cannot be separated from my Being except at death. My beliefs are in all my decision making but if I see God as part of my decision it makes a big difference how I make them. We see today a group of believer who have distorted the beliefs of a religion because of anger as war rages in the Middle East. Where is the anger coming from? Fear, not love of self or others. Hitler feared the Jews. He saw the Jew as imperious to which he became. We might say that Hitler created the Jews and the Jews created a Hitler. Try to figure that one mystery out. God does not have favorites and is not on anyone's side. Everyone is a child of God's so let's move into a healthier means of negotiations the differences of beliefs. Mine is not better than yours just different. We are all trying to define life and God or there is no reason to be on planet earth. Negotiations are only possible if power and control are taken out of the equation. We all need to start the changes with no need to power over anything except our own lives. Churches, parenting, marriages and etc. need to stop the need to power over as they are not good skills in any of these relationships. Youth have left the church as they see it not making much difference in the world today. We need to lessen to them more and set up more teen discussion groups. I-ley have a lot of wisdom that is not tapped into. I loved my children's teen years after all they were taking what I had taught them and using it or expounding on it. The root of much of the power over came about from a male dominate society instead of a God centered society. as "It"/ God never made any power over for we have free will to over ride God's desire for our life. Free will is unconditional love in a design. Sin is not against God but against the highest design for your life which is using your God given talents. So you sin against self. Not living up to potential not as right or wrong as you have eternity to get there but as a chance to be all you can be now. Most live life in the comfort zone and fear taking risks. We call risks that did not produce what we intended; mistakes when they are learning growing experiences. In groups I led I told the group that I did not make mistakes, I just had learning growing experiences. See the differences in emotions around risks through changing your thinking?

The devil did not make me do it as there is no devil. An omnipotent God does not need an adversary meaning an all powerful God does not need a foe. "It" can handle what it created just fine. See these were the contradiction in religion that really bothered me enough to send me on the quest for the truth. I am just sharing here what is the truth for me today as it is being expounded upon all the time. %ere are not enough libraries to hold all of the truths as none of us has but a speck of it.

Remember I said Hitler created the Jews and the Jews created a Hitler; well we created the bombing of the world trade center. WHAT? Take responsibility for it happening? What affects one affects all. We are all one. Our responsibility is in making our fellow mankind angry enough to go to such drastic measures as to strike out at what they think is the root cause of their problems. Our none exceptions of others beliefs are the root cause of the anger at us. I believe there were many who believed that we should not have gone to war but oil was the cause and fear used as an opportunity to advance the few War is hell. Look at it and see the turn around in the need for oil right now. Alternatives have become more desirable and affordable. Now these are my observations but oil producing countries are having their own issues right now So was it worth the war or stirring up other religious peoples or factions of religions that made the problem worse not solving a thing but moving us ahead in not needing to be so dependent on oil. Maybe we are seeing what goes around comes around? When you hurt others you are really hurting self. We are all one! The bases of all is anger. We need to stop making people angry because we do not accept their differences. Negotiation is still the way to a civilized world. Money is not evil but people can be and the use of it is sometimes. We are a bankrupt country and will have to pay for getting there.

I always had a problem with the media when they said that they did not understand the wars, shootings in schools, the street riots and even peaceful marches, as the answer was anger and no one wanted to talk about that as it took the responsibility back to all of us. We need to see our responsibility in letting people get so angry that they fight back the only way they know how. How to outsmart your opponent can be left to peaceful means like negotiations. When raising my children, one of the strategies was to help them find their own solutions. Culturally we think we have the answer for others.

I never felt that I fit into this world but was taught that it was ok not to be normal, "who wanted to be normal? (Did I tell you that I had one of the best parents going?) When norms were ever changing and some just did not make sense. "Survival of the fittest!" No! The fittest should be taking care of the those less fortune. Why do you think there are different color of skin, different talents, different physical appearances, and different abilities? So we can all have purpose and meaning. We need to make sure everyone is heard and valued. Unfairness is always going to produce anger. Success needs to be redefined as I said before. My parents were very successful and never had two dimes to rub together. Their success as I see it was in wisdom. I still marvel at their answers to my issues. My Dad died of farm related asthma at 57. When he was told that he needed to move off the farm, the only thing he knew and loved, he sat us all down and told us, that he would rather die early than give up farming and we agreed with him. Of course moving to

Arizona was not to any of our likings. Mom died at 88 and was wisdom abound. She had nine living children and when asked why she had so many, she said, "What one would you have liked me to have eliminated". We never asked that question again. We were allowed a voice with respect, and mine was at times testy. I always had a million questions. My siblings got told by me what was right and wrong and I was a pain. That is why I never fit in as I was a preacher even back then. Try did not want to hear from me how to live their life and I do not blame them. As for me I did not know any better as I was very black or white. I wanted to be a good parent like my parents so stayed home to raise my children and I am glad I did as it was a good growing time for me and I do believe I have unique children, as they are humanitarians. They taught me more than I taught them for if you are aware in life the experiences help you learn and grow. They are all fascinating characters, two sons and a deceased daughter. I will write about my daughter later, who was a fascinating character who did not like planet earth and let me know that at an early age. She died at 31 and felt she never fit in as she would say time and again that, people just did not get it. I m sure she did not get it in many ways too, namely how to deal with the craziness here on planet earth.

We are sheep to slaughter as we want to fit in when we should be taught that being our own person is far more normal as we were created with endless possibilities and should feel free to develop any number of them. Try everything that you want to see where your interest or talent really are. Everyone has the built in need to be happy at what they do but get stuck in fear and economics. I have had three major jobs in life and loved each one; the airlines, parenting and psychotherapist. I am not unique or rather I should not be for if we would slow down and ponder life more and had people around us that encouraged us to be adventurous we would find our nitch and be happier.

Common core is so the wrong way to go in fostering individuality Cookie cutter kids is not God intended!

If you are not knowledgeable enough to create a solution then ask for help. Why do foreign students do better than our own with the same studies? It is in the parenting and teaching. The enter action with the parents is very encouraging and parents are involved in studies not sports and dragging children to this or that. Not that outside activities are not important but not to the degree that our culture has become. What is the biggest money making industry in America? It is sports. So we got children chasing after something that they will never likely use. A waste of time and money. Go sit under a tree and read a book together.

Our educational system is our demise, as it can only produce some pretty ugly stuff, like anger, higher drop outs, loneliness, competition, depression and the feeling of something is missing as it is. We are not all alike and success is not a piece of paper. Refine success and draw out of each child what they are capable off with out making it less important than another ascribed belief of what is success.

Who should be paid the most as a career? Teachers! After my children left the house it was the teacher that I depended on for influencing my child. Hillary Clinton wrote a book, "It Takes a Village to Raise a Child".

So how did we go wrong in not paying teacher more? It became a women's job as rightfully it should as females have better traits for the job, but we lived in a male dominant society and it was not a fair or intelligent society. So who is in charge has long been astray. As common core was not well thought out and blatantly so for the person or people did not know God or human behavior. See why we are sheep to slaughter. This blunder just astounds me.

A side note while I am on astounds me; is why someone has not stopped this horrifying election campaigning demeaning circus that is going on. The media has no creditable for me and I turn to Canadian news most of the time. They try to stay out of our craziness as much as they can. It is going to be our demise as we have lost more of out creditability. The good news is that Hillary will win and a lot of women are not ready to be governed by women but this will help them get there. Bad things happen for a good reason. Republican party is washed up and exposure of the corruption is just starting. Republican party is really a WASP party and they need to get over themselves. Look what they did to Obama and it has backfired. I feel sorry for Hillary already as she is going to have to face some economic bad times. Things will not be so easy to brush under the rug. If we can remember we are all one and we all helped us get there than we can all pull together to get us out. What effect one effects all. Do not follow me I am lost is so true for our culture.

Ego will fight back, not common sense or wisdom and here lies the problem with really believing there is a God. Why did "It" / God let this happen? Well "It" did not do this or let it happen. There is evil in the world and free will and it is in mankind. Evil is not in spirit or soul.

These writings are my autobiography in a sense as it is an account of what I have experienced and understand to the best of my ability. It is where I have been and who I am. I have been on alert and a seeker of the truth for 77 years now and it is always changing as it should be for all of us.

My children taught me much about the spiritual life because if you really make them a part of your life, out of the mouth of babe's come much truths until we squash it. I tried not to squash it as I had a voice when growing up. Respect was a great part of the voice. Dad had more tolerances for my voice than Mom or maybe I went to him more than Mom but we had a good working relationship. I always wanted to please him so I worked on the farm with him while Mom was busy with us kids even though she went to the barn to milk. He was quiet and reserved. A very gentle soul. Mom the disciplinarian and more with the rules as she had to be with nine kids to keep in line. We were good kids and very polite. Mom had a lot of wisdom that seemed to be built in. She was not a big talker either. My parent never sat around much and we did not have TV, no phone, and the nearest neighbor was a quarter of a mile away. You did not hear either talk about anyone in a negative way except for the facts about them. Neighbors said about my Mom, that you could eat off her floors. See why she never sat down except to feed a baby. My mom was an A student in school as in the attic of our farm house was her works and report cards. She was born in Parishville NY but grew up on Long Island for a lot of her life. Her ancestry was 1629 coming to America as a Pilgrim. My Dad was born and lived most of his life in and around Madrid, NY. His Mom was born in Morrisburg, Canada. They were French and Scottish, mostly Scottish according to my grandmother. My Dad loved animals and the farm. You could ask him for a horse and get it but a bike no. I think I made a good choice for parents and I'm a cross between the two.

This background brings me back to my experiences with my children and marriage. As I said if invested in rearing your children unselfishly and with at least some unconditional love you will take away more in your own growth and development than you dreamed. Try taught me much about the meaning of life and the spirit of living. It was more exciting than a classroom as it provided for live interaction. No dull moments. As parents my husband and I were 24/7 in parenting. Now fun is one of my favorite words as my childhood was fun, I wanted my children's to be fun. So I would mow the lawn, paint the house, clip the hedge, grocery shop, clean the driveway and anything else so my husband could have the weekend off to go have some fun mostly with the children in mind. If we went golfing, he and I, it was a 7am tee time so we could have time with the children. Before you think I am seeing it this way for my benefit; I can tell you if I was asked what I did for a living, I would say I had the best job in the world I was, "A Mom" One of my son's once said that that was not cool as other Mom's did not say that. I guess I said it too much. Remember I gave up a job with Eastern Air Lines and became a Mom both jobs I loved. Now I am a Sagittarian and remember we make lemonade out of lemons.

Church, prayer, school, reading to our children and around the table teaching took place. The round table teaching was after dinner and on subjects like sex education, religion, and giving the children a time to tell their stories and complaints. I am not sure if my children did not resent this part of their life as I noticed they did not do it with their children. It maybe took away from their play time. It was not a long discussion or teaching time. So!

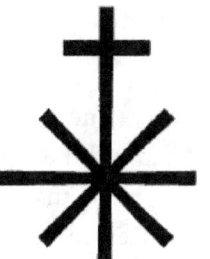

My Daughter

When my son's were 5 and 7 years of age, we went on a summer vacation to Winnipeg, Canada. I had two great Aunts and some cousins there and it was Manitoba's centennial so visited them and went on a wilderness camping trip. The wilderness camping trip was never my idea but I would have been out voted as we had a democratic family system. So off we go and it was ok as I did get to see relatives. Loved these people as they were just down to earth good people and one family were wheat farmer in the country of Sperling We stayed over night in the farm house after a steak dinner and a hymn sing alone, as one cousin was the organist for the church That night I could not sleep or was awaken by a visit from an angel. I do not know what it said. But went to sleep. My husband had gone with cousins to set up our tent at a camping site. We forged up a river for a day seeing only one person and had to portage at times. Arrived at a spot for the night, set up two tents while oldest son went fishing. He caught two nice size fish and put them on a line in the water over night but in the morning something had eaten most of them. Our dinner that

night was soup with mosquitoes as they were so thick that we got into tents right away. The next morning the mosquitoes were an inch thick on the camping stove so we know we had protein for dinner. We decided we should go back to a less dense forest so found an island that no one was on or likely had been for awhile.

lhis water was cold and crystal clear but you had to wear socks to swim as there were lots of leeches. To our surprise we had neighbors and the mainland was not far away. A family who came in by the railroad tracts invited us to a cookout one night. Our invitation was written on a piece of bark with an envelope that was laced with a strip of bark of the white birch.

How awesome was that. I still have it. It was a worth while experience and made all the adventures worth it. It was years later that I let my family know that I liked luxury vacation not camping but the experiences we had were unique. I got the say in two other vacation and that was camping near Disney World and going to Puerto Rico

Why tell this story? Well when we got home, I discovered I was pregnant. The angel must have told me I was going to have a girl as for nine months I told everyone that I was having a girl. No ultra sound back then. My family and friend voiced concern for me for they wanted to know what would I do if it was a boy. I just never entertained the thought. My life was always a close walk with God So I knew that I knew that I knew it was the desires of my heart, a daughter. My husband wanted no more children especially a girl as he was raised by three strong willed females.

I called my aunt when I found out and she was delighted and remarked that I was not the first to come to their virgin woods and get pregnant. They came to see her the summer she was born. This is a virgin story as I had not thought of the angel's visit till now. So before you think I am referring to a virgin birth Stop I believe in no virgin births as in the bible times virgin births were defined as first born of a young women. I believe God set "Its" laws in place and does not break them as there is no need too. There are mysteries that we do not understand yet but would not violate God's laws of nature. The way we use the virgin birth of Jesus is another way mankind made God human. To me the most blatant clue There are no coincidences. Everything does happen for a reason and my daughter was a strong part of my spirituality. She was born April 24,1971 at 8:15am. She was a healthy baby and the brothers loved her and I never saw any signs of jealousy or complaints. They took her under their wings and taught her games and if asked to watch after her they seemed to be ok with it all. Dad on the other hand stayed distant from her with his own issues with thinking I would favor her over the boys. His family issues were from being raised by the strong females. His mom saw no reason not to repeat many times that she never wanted him but loved him. His mom was a good person and had wisdom as flat rules but as I saw it very little knowledge of what words can do. She had lots of fears and I never felt her warm and fuzzy. I used to believe it was the English back ground.

We named our girl Christine as it had Christ in it and I was thankful for her as an addition to our family. My journey took a different turn with her birth in my drive to know God better, at night I read my Bible Now I had always kept God foremost in my life and as a family it was practiced by us all.

But when she was three months old I went to visit friends back in Connecticut where we had lived for seven years. The three children and I went as husband had to work and this as not what he would want to do for his vacation. He was not that fond or close to this family as I was. My connection was God. Now they were attending a Presbyterian church in Simsbury called, "The Barn" On Sunday morning we all went to that church and left Christine in the nursery and the two boys went with us all to the loft which was the sanctuary. The milk house was the gift shop, the silo was a solicitude prayer room to which I had prayed in the day before and found it neat. Remember I m a farmers daughter. This property was a farm given to the church now.

The sermon was given off the cuff which seemed to be just for me. When alter call was presented I found myself up front crying and everyone putting hands on me praying. I was embarrassed when it was over and confused. My friends said I had had a "born again" experience. I can tell you things were never the same but I also believe you can have many "born again" experiences as I have. This lead me on an even stronger drive to understand the universe and me. I basically told no one of the experience but these friends were there to talk to for a few years. Lost tract of them now for they seemed to not grow in the way I did and we can get to attached to the others which can keep us from exploring on our own. Remember our journeys are all unique. Before I leave these friends I want to say they lead me into the gifts of the spirit which they seemed to have some mind reading and foretelling. So called me on occasions to tell m what God wanted me to know. One very impressive experience was when I was sure that I wanted to leave my Methodist church and go to a Pentecostal church full time. She called and said God said to tell me not too. Now I was crushed and bewildered as no one knew my desires but me. I had told no one. It turned out to be good advise. Now does God give any other advice!!!

My husband was not someone I could count on for emotional support so did not try to help him understand my journey into the truth. Most men in our culture cannot be there for others in emotional support as we had squashed that with our teaching of little boys have to be John Wayne's mentality Thank God that is for the most part in the past. So he was there for our daughter mostly when she got hurt or sick. I was not good with the children when the got hurt so he would take over if he was there. Today I am a self healer and believe my issues with the medical profession is due to past lives in which I was a doctor or was maltreated by the profession. I could have also maltreated others. I could know but do not want too.

We do much of our behavior on an unconscious level so when I say they do not know any better, it is now a built in habit and not on the conscious level. It is a reaction and automatic response due to past experiences. We are reactionary due to our past experiences and that is why it is hard to let go of old thinking and beliefs. We get very comfortable with our reacting the same way all the time. Men in therapy used to say well that is the way I am and she will just have to like it. This was the old timers excuse.

Christine, my daughter was a fast learner and did everything early or there about except for walking she would not unless she had my finger. She would creep until she wanted to walk then cry for my hand. One day we were getting ready for a vacation and I was helping her Dad with the car and she wanted me to come as the sidewalk was hard on her knees. I told her she needed to get up and walk as I was busy. She did, she was just one. The neighbor saw this as we had talked about this behavior so came over and said I saw that. I guess this was the foretelling of our symbiotic relationship. This was just the beginning of her doing and saying things that really baffed me. Having time to pay attention to my children still gives me great joy and memories. The boys were teaching me so I was more prepared with her.

These baffing experiences continued to the end of her life. She had de' ja vu at 4years of age. We would go somewhere and she would say, "She remembered being here before" when she could not have she was too young. I had never been there before. This sent me on a spiritual journey as I did not know de'ja vu at all. I thought at first that the place or room we were in had just so many ways of looking so that was her experience. I had studied interior decorating when I was pregnant for her and one time I asked her why she was such a good decorator and she said, "Did not you tell me you studied it when I was in your tummy?

I always knew the voice of God, left my body knowingly each night when I was 7 and 8 years of age but her experiences left me with more questions than answers so my quest had begun, alone on my journey. I read the Bible each night and prayed for knowledge and understanding, The church was limited as I asked and talked about this experience with church members with little help. I have read the Bible cover to cover five times and studied it for 17 years. It did help to attend a Pentecostal church as they were into the gifts of the spirit more. I learned to speak in tongues, my gift of the spirit was prophecy to which I threw a fit about as they killed the prophets and I had many neat experiences. I had an out of body experience and told no one for years. had my life pass before me so I could met the times ahead. Which brings me to Christine, who said at about 7years of age, that she came to planet earth because I wanted a daughter and was not staying long I am sure I said nothing as she was a child and I forgot it until she reminded me when she was sick and dying. She had cancer off and on from 16 and died at 31. She had three different cancers and each of the first two after we were told she would say, "Mom get with the program; this is not about death and dying as God is not through with me yet." The last cancer was Ewing's Carcinoma and with that she said, "Mom get with the program as this is about dying. See I can't even get an adult cancer.'

It was through Christine and later years that I learned we script our life before coming to planet earth for certain learning or remembering. As we pass through the birthing process we are to forget the script but she remembered more than most. De'ja vu is not as uncommon as you might think, just not talked about much. We all have it happen from time to time. Mine was not de'ja vu but I would have knowledge that seemed to come from nowhere. I wake up with solutions to issues in the middle of the night or what I call sermons/revelations. All this was common in the experiences of people of the early Bible but not much taught in churches like the Baptist churches usually do not believe in the gifts of the spirit as it was for the days of old. and the rest might just as well not as teachings are limited. Again it is limited as I see it for power and control. Jesus said, "Greater things than these, you will do." He believed we would move forward but we have regressed.

Reading my Bible was fascinating as I discovered as you grew the same passage that you understood one way for sometime now told you something more that you had not seen before or understood in this new way. Well that is the key to life as everything is being expounded upon in beliefs as you are ready for new teachings. My heritage on Mom side was Quaker than Methodist and good medium for me as it allowed for changes and freedom. Life is a continuum and it is eternal. Another clue!

When the children were all in school, I went to college and got my bachelor and my masters in social work. I was still about the others but it fit my personality. The last semester of my bachelor degree, my husband and I got a divorce as he moved out of state. The boys were 17 and 15 so went with him. As a design in our journey the divorce was perfect timing as it took us all in a very different direction. Today it looks even more perfect as I needed to rediscover, Lois. I was a people pleaser, of course unconsciously so needed to spiritually see the purpose of life for the individual. Some of this was not apparent at the time and I fought with God many times as going forward made me feel all alone. Well now I know why we need to be alone. Growth and development need to be personalized and that is a lonely journey at times. I got to be ok with it for 30 years. Much of my life seems to be it, whatever it was chose me rather than My choosing it. My becoming a psychotherapist was one such choice. It just happened. My quest to find God or the truth led me to it as needing to know who we are was a part of that quest. My gift of the spirit was prophecy and psychotherapy are not that different. How? Well, defining prophecy as a prediction in peoples lives is what psychotherapy is. If change does not take place in the people life a therapist should be able to see what will or will not happen in their lives. They have a goal and you help them get there. The dictionary is one of the second most important books. One is always in sight as words used are very important. In my case English.

Language being the most misunderstood of ways to communicate. English the hardest because it has so many different meanings to the same word.

After my graduation from college, we moved to upstate New York as Christine thought we needed to be closer to family. Probably do to what lie ahead for me. She had been flying out to Dad's for three years and at thirteen decided she needed to go live with him and her brothers to see what that was like. I did not sleep for three nights as it was hard for me and I could not stop her as I knew that this was common for children to want to see the other side. It was the beginning of the end. I asked her when she was dying if I should have stopped her and she said, no it was part of the plan. She was a people pleaser so the fear and control factor became more than she could handle. Her Dad's church was Pentecostal, Her Dad was clueless, and she went to a Christian school. She was a child that in all the bad times would be the best of supports for me. She was a trooper and thought she could handle this. She also again attached herself to a minister as a father figure.

She did not get the warm fuzzy dad she thought she would. She got cancer at 16. She came home that summer and was very sick, we talked about it but again she said she could handle it. I thought she was anorexic. I knew she wanted to stay with me but that was defeat and not her. In October, I flew out to be with her during an a biopsy on a lymphoid in her neck, which took the doctors 9 months to decide to do. She made it known that it would not happen if I was not at her side. She flew back with me We did not like the treatment for her in my town as we would both have Goosebumps going to her procedures. When the doctor wanted to take bone marrow from both sides, she said no just one side was enough. The

doctor was upset and said you could die if and she said, "that Christ was her Lord and that if she was to die than so be it" There was total silence in the room and I broke it by saying Christine just let him do both sides. She was at this time weighting less than 100 pounds and it was scary. The next test was done in Syracuse and when we got finished with that we went to Florida to my sisters for treatment of three months. Just radiation and for seven years she was cured. Came home and went to college to which she did well in and for 11 years was the only place she felt herself with. Again attached herself to a professor of philosophy. She was very bright and could write well. I could see she lacked the bounce that she was in her early life. She always felt the cancer as the defeat and she had two more cancers along with other mistakes she could not shake She was hardest on herself. She married twice both disasters and both produced a boy, so with two sons and a useless husband she exits planet earth final blow for her was college as a female professor she had befriended who was Jewish turned on her as she chose to do her master thesis on, "The Meaning of Life" I read the abstract and it was brilliant but Bonnie did not like it. Christine went to the head of the department and the department head a good mentor for Christine told her to go ahead and present it. Christine was very hurt now with nothing left to fight for so got Ewing's. All these times she and I talked about her feelings and what was going on but this was a slippery slope and now unstoppable. She never complained or said, "why me" in it all. She

"It" Is God

dropped out of church but found a positive God again in Philosophy. There was no devil, hell or a need for a Dad. Thou she said she and dad had come to terms with their relationship in November before her death. I did not ask what that was as she seemed happy with it all.

I was with her when she died and it was a personal and awesome experience. Meant to be and planned by the celestial committee. She had called on Thursday night and said she could not do this anymore so was going to the hospital. I got there Friday and she was not responsive because of meds and died on Saturday never coming around. I knew she heard me Everyone was tired and left so I did her hair which she always wanted me to play with and talked with her about her beauty and to go home which she did. I did not know the exact minute she left her body but looked down to see her hands which seemed to be red checks and said, "you little stinker you are gone".I started to really cry but in seconds remembered all my beliefs in death and dying. Spent a few minutes when a knock came on the door and it was three of her friends who wanted to see her; two males and a female.

I told them they were welcome to come and say goodbye but she was gone. Then after a few minutes, I said, "I needed to tell the nurses she had died". So we went to the family room and shared some of her life.

The negative image of a father God in churches and religion or parenting is most damaging. Clue!

My letting go of Christine gave me lesson abound as no one can loose a child without God's presents in a very positive way. God had already taught me as Christine did, that death is not the end of anything but the body. If you see it all in the plan the sting has left and enlightenment comes, and awareness is there. Sad? yes but the thoughts and words used were powerful

Christine had search for answers in Philosophy and I in psychology/ Human behavior. We were looking for the truth which cannot be found in others, for it is your truth and your need. It is personal and worth it's weight in gold and beyond. It is not statig as everything is changing. I was becoming aware but to experience it is to live it, to proof it and to own it. You become the authority of your beliefs.

I tried here to share some of the spiritual aspects of our lives together. Friends and family thought that Christine would visit me in spirit but the first was in August in a dream when she said, "She was having a hard time adjusting there". That was a surprise as I thought of her as an old soul. Since then her visits were many and the most bizarre was upon getting out of the bath tub one morning, I had toweled off and noticed my tummy green. I touched it and it was like a green lipstick. My first thought was Christine. I got toilet paper and then a Kleenex and wiped it off. Still have it in a baggy. Nothing in the bathroom was green and my towel had none on it. I laughed about it all My son is a hydrogeologist and has things test for contents all the time, so called him to see if he could find out cost and if the sample could be tested. Now the still small voice said to forget it as the substance would be unknown. Being Lois, I thought let's see what he finds out. Son came back with not enough substance and too costly. Good answers. A median friend told me that spirits like to play jokes and have a good sense of humor. So be it.

It is in your face experiences that tell you there are more mystery to life than meets the eye and it is ever changing as you are ready. It never gets dull as it is in your design or script.

It seems that my family is on planet earth this time around to deal with betrayal, including me. Because we are rescuers it is easy to get betrayed as we have naive ways and trust to much and at times feel isolated due to the betrayal.

She wrote an 800 page book on a past life as a slave women which got lost after her death but that was ok. She was a good writer, so I wrote a book on "The Meaning of Life", my version in her honor. Not the way she would have written but from my point of view.

It is important that we except what is not what we would have liked it to be. helps us focus on the experience rather than wasting energy on what might have been. Living in the NOW, present moment I do not know when I slipped into the present moment living but it is freedom. Now I do not stay there all the time either but freedom is what we are searching for as I and you need to be free to be me/you. Tie intended freedom from the creator. Peeling away the layers can only be done in adulthood.

The most important aspect of peeling away the layers are; First a desire to be free of baggage and know why you came to planet earth. In finding you, you will find the others. No two people will know God the same as we all see life differently. Know that it was meant to be that way as in a design.

Secondly, You need to stop saying you will someday set aside time to be still and know God through self.

I was in church for 65 years and did not find God as I know today. We all have very busy lives so finding time and prioritizing is of the utmost importance.

Thirdly; Seek unconditional love. You might say that this is first and foremost but you cannot go there without process some of self and God. You are priority, the opposite from some church teachings. Knowing self to know others or love your neighbor as yourself, is pointing to loving self as the priority. Many churches had the people looking to the others when all the time it was about finding the self. Fear and control again the issue.

I was the odd kid out when growing up and maybe today but it strengthens character not take away from it. We need to stop thinking we can stop bullying as another way will just take it's place but stop the abusive behavior. Teach that you are bullied because you are loved, stop reacting to it and know that it prepares you more realistically for the real world. Stop reacting and it will go away. Dissect the bulling with the person to see why that person takes it personally then you can help that person grow. My parents taught me that years ago and were very wise, not an ounce of common sense to be found today. When was it said that we have perfect world? What does not kill you makes you stronger I was told.

There is no time to parent today as everyone is eking out a living and exhausted. We can all make the changes needed if we all want the same thing. Stop the world I want to get off is powerful stuff not in death but before death. Just make a difference now. We have that much power, read about the walls of Jericho. It is about being of one mind. Ihe remains of Jericho prove that the walls fell in.

One of my favorite songs is, "Make the world go away'

Throw out the schedule and just let go; mediate, pray, and just be still. "Be still and know that I am God."

Hear that still small voice.

So have the desire, make time and seek unconditional love.

The most important ingredient in life is people and how we treat self and each other.

www.ingramcontent.com/pod-product-compliance
Lightning Source LLC
LaVergne TN
LVHW011950070526
838202LV00054B/4883